"Lacy Finn Borgo has thought more deeply and practiced more fully Jesus' words inviting us to 'become like little children' than just about anyone I know. And now with *Faith Like a Child* she has brought this vast reservoir of wisdom to us. In helping us 're-member our childhood selves' Lacy gently guides us into a more joy-filled life . . . indeed, into a life more like Jesus. I am delighted."

Richard J. Foster, founder of Renovaré and author of *Celebration of Discipline* and *Learning Humility*

"With a delightful sense of humor, which often brought tears to my eyes, and a profound wisdom of the heart shaped by the wonders and wounds of her own pilgrimage through life, Lacy Finn Borgo invites readers to welcome their own childhood self. As we follow her carefully crafted suggested practices, she helps us to discover what it may mean to live with the faith of a child. We realize afresh that we can never ever be separate from the Great Love who knitted us together in our mother's womb and who hasn't put down those knitting needles ever since. Most especially, Lacy Borgo's words help us to know ever more deeply the truth of Jesus' words that, unless we become like children, we will not experience the joyful realities of God's presence within our everyday lives."

Trevor Hudson, author of *Discovering Your Spiritual Identity: Practices for God's Beloved* and *Seeking God: Finding Another Kind of Life with St. Ignatius and Dallas Willard*

"My friend Lacy Borgo writes with wit, wisdom, and a wonderful Texas drawl. Her latest book, *Faith Like a Child*, explores childhood as a wisdom way for stepping inside the here-and-now kingdom of eternal friendship with God. I hope you will read this book with the openness of a child, playfully try on each of the welcoming practices she suggests, and be attentive to the Spirit's healing of any childhood wounds that might hinder your ability to hear Jesus' welcoming invitation to play."

Gary W. Moon, founding executive director of the Martin Institute for Christianity and Culture and the Dallas Willard Center for Christian Spiritual Formation at Westmont College

"Lacy Finn Borgo explodes the myth that spiritual growth is stuffy. With her trademark wit, sly observation, and earthy humor, Lacy invites us to go deeper with God by remembering all the strengths children bring to exploring the with-God life. Who knows? Maybe you'll start encountering God again, laughing and playing with him instead of just thinking about him!"

Ted Harro, president of Renovaré

"In my lifetime I have never witnessed a moment when the virtue of humility was more needed for the Christian community. Lacy Borgo's *Faith Like a Child* wisely and beautifully invites us to rediscover this lost virtue by recapturing wonder and reclaiming our identity as God's beloved children. I highly recommend this timely and significant contribution to the spiritual formation movement by my friend and doctoral professor."

Dave Ripper, lead pastor of Crossway Christian Church and coauthor of *The Fellowship of the Suffering*

"Who would have known that formation into Christlikeness could be so fun? In *Faith Like a Child*, author and spiritual director Lacy Borgo uses Scripture, poetry, and personal stories to invite us to see ourselves as the light-hearted children we were created to be. A helpful framework for understanding Christian spiritual formation, this book is one I recommend to anyone seeking to grow in embracing God as our Mothering Father."

Kurtley Knight, assistant professor of spiritual formation at George Fox University's Portland Seminary

"Reading *Faith Like a Child* is like sitting with Lacy Finn Borgo at her kitchen table, drinking iced tea, and watching beloved children play—not just our own children and the neighbors' kids but also the little ones we used to be. She reminds us of what we once knew about the world and the Holy. She reminds us of wonder, safety, freedom, and delight—and then she helps us enter those moments in our lives today. This book is a gift from a mother who sees the world through a lens of grace and gives us a new vision for our lives."

Linda Taylor, Episcopal priest and spiritual director

"*Faith Like a Child* is the most practical examination of a childlike faith I have ever encountered. Lacy Finn Borgo's words are grounded and honest as she paints a beautiful picture of a dynamic faith even in the midst of a chaotic world. I found in these pages a profoundly winsome, tender-hearted invitation to let go of my desire for control and be free to roll in the mud and fully embrace the One who calls me beloved."

Jason Feffer, pastor of The Practice church

Faith Like a Child

EMBRACING OUR LIVES AS
CHILDREN *of* GOD

LACY FINN BORGO

An imprint of InterVarsity Press
Downers Grove, Illinois

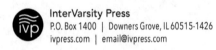
InterVarsity Press
P.O. Box 1400 | Downers Grove, IL 60515-1426
ivpress.com | email@ivpress.com

InterVarsity Press® is the publishing division of InterVarsity Christian Fellowship/USA®.
For more information, visit intervarsity.org.

Scripture quotations, unless otherwise noted, are from the New Revised Standard Version Bible,
copyright © 1989 National Council of the Churches of Christ in the United States of America.
Used by permission. All rights reserved worldwide.

While any stories in this book are true, some names and identifying information may have been changed
to protect the privacy of individuals.

Excerpts from chapter 8 were first published in Spiritual Directors International's journal, *Presence*,
vol. 27, no. 4.

The publisher cannot verify the accuracy or functionality of website URLs used in this book
beyond the date of publication.

Cover design: David Fassett
Interior design: Jeanna Wiggins

ISBN 978-1-5140-0398-5 (print) | ISBN 978-1-5140-0399-2 (digital)

Printed in the United States of America ♾

Library of Congress Cataloging-in-Publication Data
A catalog record for this book is available from the Library of Congress.

30   29   28   27   26   25   24   23 | 12   11   10   9   8   7   6   5   4   3   2   1

To my wild, wonderful, wounded,

and on-the-way-to-healing family.

WE HAVE

LEARNED TO LOVE,

TOGETHER.

Contents

Introduction

Welcoming the Child Within

It's important to know the way to enter when visiting my parents. From the driveway, all you can see is the garage. But if you enter that garage and weave through the cars, tools, and unimaginable array of glass canning jars, you'll see a staircase at the back leading to a humble door. Over that door is a ceramic sign that reads "Bienvenidos a casa de los abuelos." In English, the sign—a nod to their Texas roots and my mother's love of Mexican culture— reads, "Welcome to the grandparents' house." If you take these grandparents up on their welcome and enter that door, you might feel like you've come home. For they'll be grandparents to you, as they are to everyone they know. Children and adults far and wide call them Big Mama and Grand. They embody the word *welcome*.

The word *welcome* comes to us from the eighth century and means "a wished-for guest." The word itself combines two parts: "to will or desire" and "to come." Woven within the word is an acknowledgment of the will to choose the presence of another. Welcome then requires an intentional action, a literal coming together of those who have been separate.

Welcome can be found throughout Scripture, both in the Hebrew Scriptures and in the New Testament. In Genesis, God welcomed—that is, desired and then acted on that desire—the world into existence. Eve welcomed Adam into human intimacy. God welcomed Abraham into friendship. Joshua welcomed a nation into a home. Rahab welcomed strangers into freedom. Ruth welcomed her mother-in-law into the family. Samuel welcomed God into speech. Mary welcomed God into her body. And Jesus? Jesus is all welcome. The Gospels tell us that Jesus welcomed women, men, and children into a way of being that birthed new life. The welcome that Jesus continues to offer reweaves all that we once thought separate.

Our welcomes are all connected: how we welcome our childhood selves is connected to how much we welcome the children in front of us, which is connected to how much we welcome the Christ child. And to welcome the Christ child is to welcome humanity itself. Children are the most human among us. They are the most present, most authentic, and most connected with the least effort and intention.

The incarnation is the foundation for the holy act of becoming human. Jesus' life showed us that each developmental stage can be a place of holy delight. He was a child who did childlike and childish things. In him was the delight, awe, and wonder of discovery. He who knew all things experienced them afresh with a human body. He experienced life as an infant, a toddler, a child, a tween, and an adolescent. He encountered the same fears and worries and existential questions that we do.

As we welcome our own childhood selves, we welcome the humanity of Jesus. And in that welcoming, we find a companion for life. And further, when we welcome our own childhood selves and the Christ child, we will be more able to welcome children in our own lives. The act of welcoming involves a presence filled with acceptance, compassion, and empathy. When we feel with others and accept them, our level of desire for connection deepens. When our childhood memories hold places of fear and rejection, we wall off our childhood selves, and our welcome to children suffers.

BECOMING LIKE CHILDREN

Back when my children were very young and my soul was lonely, I gathered a group of women once a month in my home for dinner and a book discussion. Dinner was on my grandmother's fine china, and the food was Colorado luxurious, plenty of it and hearty for winter, worth lingering over for hours. Some of us found childcare, others brought their littles. I remember a random comment made while chatting at the dining room table.

"When Jesus said, 'You must become like children to enter the kingdom of God,' surely he didn't mean that," one mother said, pointing to her son—who was picking his nose and wiping it on my couch. We all laughed that kind of laugh that said, "We hear you, sister, and thank God that's your kid."

We are made for experiencing God. Our first and most natural inclination as children is to connect with God in deeply uniting yet often ordinary ways. We adults have much to learn. This book will explore what it looks like to re-member (to revisit and revive what has been part of us) our childhood selves, to let the Spirit heal the childhood wounds that have calloused our hearts. We will re-member the natural patterns of our childhood selves that enabled us to live with freedom in God's wonder-filled presence. We will unpack seven general ways of being that are natural to childhood and suggest healing spiritual practices that can help us grow a whole life with God. We will begin by exploring a shape of spiritual formation that addresses both the wonder we were born with and the wounds that could use some tender care. We will revisit what it looks like to develop a healthy attachment to God and how to cultivate that attachment through play, imagination, creativity, wonder, humor, and simply paying attention.

Each of us must do this essential work, and especially those of us who work or live with children—because children can spot a fake at fifty paces. We can only accompany children where we have gone. If we haven't re-membered our childhood selves, the distance between ourselves and the children in front of us will grow.

CHILDHOOD AS A WISDOM WAY

"Aunt Polly, would you tell me one of your earliest memories?" I asked while shoveling Milky Way cake into my mouth as fast as possible—I needed a free hand to take notes.

"That's a hard one . . . let me think," she replied. Even well into her nineties, her mind was as sharp as her cane.

Family reunions in the Ringener (my mom's side of the family) way are mainly about cake. There might be brisket, and various versions of potato salad, but there will always be cake. And there will be stories, tall Texas tales that are mostly true. The story I heard that day from my great-aunt Polly stirred something deep in me. I was just beginning to wonder about our early experiences of God and those tender memories that we hold dear throughout our lives: the memories that we may never tell another soul, but that we tell ourselves during hard times, when our knees become wobblier than we'd like.

She reminisced to me:

I remember it was a gray day, and I knew it had been raining because there was mud puddles everywhere. My mama had died, and on this day they were burying her. Her casket was in the back of the wagon and all the adults were walking behind it to the cemetery. I wasn't more than four or five years old, so I was playin' in the water, jumpin' in the puddles. I heard one of the aunties say, "Poor little girl, don't even know her mama died." I overheard her and thought, "I know my Mama is safe with God." I wasn't sad and I wasn't scared.

When I first heard this, I too easily dismissed her experience, falling into the same assumptions as the aunties, thinking she didn't understand the gravity of the situation. It's true that children don't fully understand death, but maybe they know more about God than adults have previously understood. Could it be that Polly already encountered God in her young life? Could it be that overheard snippets of Jesus stories enlivened her imagination and cultivated a connection with God? Maybe little five-year-old Polly understood what was necessary for the moment. Maybe her young faith held her in that knowing.

ENGAGING THIS BOOK

In this book we will be exploring the ways of children and reengaging with our own memories of childhood. Do be gentle with yourself. Some memories that come into the light of Christ might be full of delight and forgotten joy, but some might remind you of wounds long buried. Walk gently and let the Spirit lead. Deep healing of tender places can't be rushed or ramrodded. Go slow, go easy.

At the end of each chapter is a smorgasbord of practices to reunite you with your childhood self and the eternal one who loved you into being. Choose one practice, dear friend, and let it work deeply into who you are. There is no such thing as spiritual Olympics, and anyone who tells you differently is selling you something. (Yes, I know you bought this book. The stick in my eye is quite bothersome.) You can return to the other practices at a later time. My hope is that you will wander through these practices over and over for the next two decades, just long enough to grow young again.

Two tips as you begin: first, be around children. If you don't live with any, you can volunteer to teach the children at your church, or volunteer to help a child learn to read in an after-school program, or volunteer to babysit for some tired-looking parents you know. I can describe children's unique ways of being and offer strategies for you to live out these ways, but spending time with children will lead you much deeper. I'm a better typist, but they know the way by heart. Simple observation and engagement will go a long way. Second, find a traveling companion—a soul friend who can listen and help you to hear yourself and God. These friends will stay with us in the hard spots and celebrate our gains. A formal relationship of this kind is called spiritual direction; if you are looking for a less formal listening partner, feel free to ask a trusted friend.[1] This partner doesn't need to sort us out or coddle us. We only need someone to hold a safe and welcoming space for us and listen with a compassionate heart. (You can show them the previous sentence—as a gentle guide.) A helpful question to live with might be, "I wonder what you notice happening within yourself?"

And now, in the words of every child I know, "Let's play!"

1

Knowing God, Accepting Self

Focusing on God while failing to know ourselves deeply
may produce an external form of piety, but it will always
leave a gap between appearance and reality.

DAVID G. BENNER

It can be hard to hear the quiet voices of the children in the noisy dining hall at Haven House, a transitional facility for families without homes. It is a large, open space that functions much like a thoroughfare for folks walking between private rooms and the kitchen. Still, it was the best spot that we could find to paint our prayers with watercolors. I sat in a circle with a dozen or so children and asked a simple question: "What is God like?"

No hands shot up immediately. They sat for a bit in wiggly silence, while I wondered if they were bored or just distracted. Jessica answered first, "He's like big and up there [pointing to the ceiling] and, you know, watching us." Carlos chimed in, "Like, you know, Jesus." And then his sister Amelia said, "Or Mary. God is like Mary." Then Leslie began, "Once when I was outside and looking at the clouds, I saw a big storm come in, and I think God is like that. A big storm."

Each child jumped in with their own stories and thoughts about God. Like a grandmother, like a wizard, like a protector, like a friend.

WHAT IS GOD LIKE?

In his book *Cry of Wonder,* Jesuit priest and spiritual director Gerard Hughes writes that the question "What is God like?" is the question he lived his whole life.[1] This question pulses underneath our everyday living and rises to the surface when we experience the intensity of pain, suffering, joy, and love. And it is in childhood that we begin to ask this question, whether consciously or unconsciously. The question is interwoven with our fundamental questions around attachment and safety. The adults who hold the power to keep us safe and healthy also shape our pictures of God. (Yep, we've likely got more than one picture.)

Parents, grandparents, pastors, teachers, and family friends all contribute to our pictures of God. This imprinting can be a good thing when adults keep us safe and healthy. But when they don't care for us well, our picture of God gets crapped up. *Crapped up* is a West Texas term that means something was good in the beginning, but layers of cast-off muck covered up the good. It doesn't destroy what was originally there, but the first masterpiece is marred.

Safe and healthy connections with adults are not the only influences that form our picture of God. God longed us into being and then scattered divine fingerprints as invitations to connect within nature, within our own curiosity, within experiences of awe, beauty, and unity. When as children we encounter the Spirit's invitations, the question "What is God like?" reverberates in our souls.

So, what *is* God like? After completing a doctor of ministry in spiritual formation and having ongoing conversations with this divine One for fifty years, you'd think I might have this sorted out. Each time I get close to a neat definition, God blows the sides off my tidy box.

For much of Christian history we have thought of God as male, and we have used male pronouns and masculine characteristics. And while the biblical record testifies to a masculine description of God, masculine is not the only description. The biblical record also testifies to a feminine description of God. Sadly, seeing God as only masculine is limiting, harmful, and woefully inaccurate. The Bible is more expansive than that. In Genesis, we read that God made human beings in God's image, both male and female. We notice that *ruah*, the Hebrew word for God's Spirit, is feminine. This feminine answer to "What is God like?" can be found throughout Scripture.[2]

Jesus—who is the answer to the question "What is God like?"—told parables comparing God to a woman. God is like a woman who is determined to find a lost coin that is most precious to her (Luke 15:8-10). God is like a woman who hides the yeast of the kingdom of God in bread (Matthew 13:33). God is like a mother hen who longs to protect her young (Matthew 23:37). As my friend Jean Nevills likes to say, "God is our Mothering Father. God is our divine parent."

In his book *Discovering Our Spiritual Identity,* pastor, author, and spiritual director Trevor Hudson writes, "If we want to get our picture of God clearer, we must look in the direction of Jesus. . . .

Every idea and assumption that we have about God must be measured against the person of Jesus."[3] If we want to know what God is like, we need to find out what Jesus was like.

Jesus embraced himself as a child of his *Abba*. We see this in the Lord's Prayer (Matthew 6:5-15; Luke 11:1-13). He could have addressed God in this particular prayer as King, Teacher, Ruler, but he didn't. He calls out to God using a tender, familial term that acknowledges a particular relationship of belonging—divine parent and child. Jesus too was a child who lived from the wisdom of childhood; in fact, this childlike prayer shows us that he never left his childhood, but even as an adult knew how to perpetually re-member. Jesus is both older than time itself and younger than a heartbeat of the present.

If we learn, like Jesus, to re-member our childhood selves, we will find greater capacity to connect with God's presence and his kingdom (Mark 10:13-16). As our capacity expands, so does our sense of belonging to the trinitarian community of love (Luke 18:15-17). We read in 1 John 4 that God is love, but somehow, in our innermost selves, we knew that already. When our father passes on the sixth piece of pie in a room of seven people, when an aunt shows up for our basketball game, when a family friend sends us a package while we are deployed, when a teacher takes time out of her lunch to teach us prepositions, when a stranger offers a word of kindness, we know that the essence of life is love. The unfathomable mystery of it all is that God is love.

What is God like? We are invited to follow the answers to this question for all of our lives. Like lovers continually growing in the knowledge of each other, God invites us from our very beginning to fall into love. However, living with the question "What is God like?" will lead us to another: "What are we like?"

WHAT ARE WE LIKE?

By most accounts, there are eight passages in the Gospels where children are mentioned. Six specific written accounts holding two distinct stories are found in the Synoptic Gospels, Luke, Mark, and Matthew.

> An argument arose among them as to which one of them was the greatest. But Jesus, aware of their inner thoughts, took a little child and put it by his side, and said to them, "Whoever welcomes this child in my name welcomes me, and whoever welcomes me welcomes the one who sent me; for the least among all of you is the greatest." (Luke 9:46-48)

> Then they came to Capernaum; and when he was in the house he asked them, "What were you arguing about on the way?" But they were silent, for on the way they had been arguing with one another about who was the greatest. He sat down, called the twelve, and said to them, "Whoever wants to be first must be last of all and servant of all." Then he took a little child and put it among them; and taking it in his arms, he said to them, "Whoever welcomes one such child in my name welcomes me, and whoever welcomes me welcomes not me but the one who sent me." (Mark 9:33-37)

> At that time the disciples came to Jesus and asked, "Who is the greatest in the kingdom of heaven?" He called a child, whom he put among them, and said, "Truly, I tell you, unless you change and become like children, you will never enter the kingdom of heaven. Whoever becomes humble like this child is the greatest in the kingdom of heaven. Whoever welcomes one such child in my name welcomes me." (Matthew 18:1-5)

This story reflects the disciples' pecking war for power. The disciples were an ethnically oppressed people, systematically robbed of power and the simple dignity of being human. So, signing up for this outfit stirred their hopes of a new earthly ruling kingdom. They wanted to be sure that they would be part of the powerful top brass. In contrast, knowing that a child's primary concern is connection, not power, Jesus brought a child into their midst and said, "Be humble, like this." Jesus knew that what they needed was a deep connection to their identity as children of God.[4]

All three passages contain the word *welcome*. Feel free to go back and count the instances of the word. When we welcome the child in front of us or the child within us, we welcome God.

Many of us didn't receive this kind of welcome as children. If that is true of you, please remember that Jesus' invitation of welcome is eternal. Even as you read this sentence, your childhood self is being welcomed by our Mothering Father. Your core identity is as a welcomed child within the trinitarian community of love.

Let's look together at a second story, where we see something a little different unfold.

> People were bringing even infants to him that he might touch them; and when the disciples saw it, they sternly ordered them not to do it. But Jesus called for them and said, "Let the little children come to me, and do not stop them; for it is to such as these that the kingdom of God belongs. Truly I tell you, whoever does not receive the kingdom of God as a little child will never enter it." (Luke 18:15-17)

> People were bringing little children to him in order that he might touch them; and the disciples spoke sternly to them. But when Jesus saw this, he was indignant and said to them,

"Let the little children come to me; do not stop them; for it is to such as these that the kingdom of God belongs. Truly, I tell you whoever does not receive the kingdom of God as a little child will never enter it." And he took them up in his arms, laid his hands on them and blessed them. (Mark 10:13-16)

Then little children were being brought to him in order that he might lay his hands on them and pray. The disciples spoke sternly to those who brought them; but Jesus said, "Let the little children come to me, and do not stop them; for it is to such as these that the kingdom of heaven belongs." And he laid his hands on them and went on his way. (Matthew 19:13-15)

In the first story, Jesus welcomes the children, shifting the power dynamics to make space, and opening his arms wide to their full presence. But in this second story, Jesus invites us, the adults, to the humble posture of a learner. For adults, this way of the child must be learned again; it must be recovered, and it's going to require humility. This story expands to commend the child's naturally humble posture. Anchorite Maggie Ross connects humility to the capability to perceive love and enter into a deep state of communion with God. She writes, "The ability to see this love depends on our receptivity to the gift of humility, which is contemplation, purity of heart, and peace all rolled into one, the single virtue of which the paradoxes of the Beatitudes speak."[5]

All human beings come into this world in a humble state. We are not only poor in spirit, we are poor in pocket. As newborns, we mourn for the warmth, safety, and comfort of the womb. Our early grief places us in the meekest of all human states. We are hungry and thirsty to receive the gentle goodness of others. We are merciful beyond measure, willing to forgive again and again those who cannot or will not meet our needs. Our hearts begin in the simple purity of the heavens, and we are literally wired for a peacemaking that leads to secure community.[6] Without one drop of chosen, conscious attention, we as infants lived from a state of connection and wonder.

Children possess a natural, unique to them, connective consciousness. It has not been chosen or even cultivated through hours of meditation or psychedelic trips. Instead, the plasticity of the developing brain offers connective wonder through a lack of previous experiences and an innocent openness to the world. God has wired each and every one of us for this. In his book *Becoming Like a Child*, Jerome Berryman writes, "Children are not easily tempted by evil, because they remain in touch with small pleasures as well as their neighbor's pain and the excitement of learning new things about a better way to live."[7]

The previously cited passages from Luke and Mark tell us that "whoever does not receive the kingdom of God as a little child will never enter it." Matthew says that "it is to such as these that the kingdom of heaven belongs." Beyond their lack of concern over power, beyond their born state of humility, children possess a contemplative posture all their own. The contemplation of these *mini mystics*, a term I like to use to describe children and their natural connection to God, includes a wonder-filled receptivity to whatever is before them. They are not bound by systems of certainty but are free to welcome mystery in all its unknowing. They exist in a perpetual state of awe, expanding their minds, bodies, and spirits for wide-open engagement. Mini mystics are free from the judgments and crusty patterns of thinking that tend to mire adults.

The kingdom of heaven is the home of children. It is where the dimensions of both heaven and earth come together in unity with the sacred. For children, this state of connective contemplation is commonplace. Adults may find it unfamiliar, but since every person at some point was a child, the contemplative wonder-way of the child is somewhere within us. And in fact, we are all still children at some level.

Theologians and preachers far and wide, from Mike Yaconelli to Hans Urs von Balthasar, have analyzed these Gospel passages. Theologian Karl Rahner, in his treatise on a theology of childhood, proposed that human spiritual development is not bound to stages. We do not have a childhood spirituality and then trade up for an adolescent spirituality and then again trade up for a young adult spiritualty and so on. No, Rahner explained, we carry both our childhood selves and our adolescent selves with us into adulthood.[8]

We may set aside our childish ways, but what is formed in childhood is still with us; both that early state of contemplation and our childhood blessings and wounds are still present and shaping and shifting how we experience God. And how we experience God is how we experience others and the whole world. The work of adulthood is thus bound up in welcoming our childhood selves, allowing the healing of our childhood wounds, reclaiming our earliest experiences with God, and re-membering the child in us who continues to search for connection.

ALWAYS CHILDREN

Our truest identity is as a child of God. We will age and we may mature, but we are always children of God. In the final chapter of John, Jesus encounters his disciples one more time. They are (unsuccessfully) fishing and he's making breakfast on the shore. When he calls out to them, he calls them children. I wonder if Jesus was reminding them of what they knew when they were children. I wonder if he was reminding them of the times he brought a child into their midst and taught them what was most important.

Jenny, a dear friend, shared a story with me over iced tea one afternoon. The first experience of God she could remember was while jumping on the trampoline at her grandparents' house. She loved the feel of the wind in her hair, the power and dynamic energy that catapulted her into the sky. She felt wild and free and safe. At home though, her dad worked a lot and wasn't able to connect with her. Her mother, it seemed to Jenny, preferred to lavish attention on her brother. And for a long time she thought God was like them: too busy to connect with her and preferring boys rather than girls.

Still, Jenny could never shake the feeling that maybe God was something like the energy and power that catapulted her into the sky. She wondered if God was safe and wild and free, ready and willing to meet her in the strength of her own legs and launch her into the open. The contrast between her experiences with the adults in her life and what she experienced was a question that seemed to come to the surface in times of joy and excitement.

When as a young adult, she read in John 4 about Jesus' encounter with the Samaritan woman at the well, she was shocked to see his acceptance for this woman, and the wild, free power Jesus gave the woman to share the good news she'd discovered. The Spirit—the Holy Knitter, who unravels and reknits what is misshapen or broken—unknotted and loosened Jenny's picture of God that did not reflect God's true nature. Then carefully, the

Spirit took the threads of John 4, the images and words surrounding it, and wove it with Jenny's experience on the trampoline all those years ago—and a new picture emerged.

Welcoming Practices

Reflect on your picture of God. Think back to the adults in your life whose task it was to provide safety and healthy flourishing. What aspect of your picture of God did these adults shape? What aspect of your picture of God could use the tender attention of the Holy Knitter? Try praying the simple prayer "God, what are you like?" or "God, show me how I am your child."

Get curious. Write the question, What is God like? on an index card and place it in a spot that you can see frequently. Actively live with this question. Intentionally ask this question in everyday places and circumstances that might not seem particularly "religious." Jesus used bread and a lost coin to ask the question. How might reflecting on traffic, sibling squabbles, a demanding work situation, the family pet, or making dinner offer you an answer to What is God like?

Learn from a book. Reading and reflecting on children's books is an excellent way to welcome the child within and make space for the Spirit to reshape our life. The book *Images of God for Young Children* by Marie-Helene Delval and Barbara Nascimbeni can help us get in touch with the many reflections of God that surround us. Spend a full month in this lovely little book and see how your picture of God opens up. Meanwhile, if you are sensing an invitation to discover God as mother, consider reading *Mother God* by Teresa Kim Pecinovsky and Khoa Le. It is beautifully illustrated and rooted in Scripture.

17

2

Remembering Wonder, Redeeming Wounds

Always allow your childlike wonder, joy, gratitude,
love, and laughter to serve as your own soul's
tool kit for life's most difficult challenges.

JAN PORTER

I remember the rough feel of upholstery on my cheek while waking up in the front seat of my parents' pickup truck. The warmth inside made me want to go back to sleep. Instead, I sat up and looked around to find that I was alone. I remember starting to cry and standing up in the seat to look out of the passenger window. I could see my parents and a few other people gathered in a small semicircle. Everyone was crying, especially my mother; I remember feeling very sad, and then, afraid.

I carried this memory with me, but never spoke of it during my childhood. At first, I assumed it was the funeral of my infant younger sister, Charity Day, who died of whooping cough. But my mother would later tell me that I was not present at Charity's funeral. So, this must have been a time when she and my father visited her gravesite. The memory itself was not wounding, but it was a memory marker for the pain and loss for which I had no words or understanding.

This wound festering in my young life felt like abandonment and came to look like the relentless pursuit to belong. My parents were in the throes of grief while still needing to care for me, their living child. They tried to manage their pain and connect, but somehow I felt alone and without place. I have spent nearly five decades trying to reconcile with my sense of abandonment. When my wounds weep the loudest, I will beg, borrow, or steal to find belonging.

In hindsight, it makes sense that my first recollected experience of God was in nature, a place where connections are innate. Just a few years after Charity died, I felt God's presence and welcome in a grove of aspen trees. It was an incredibly ordinary experience of a child playing in the autumn leaves. There was a moment in my playing where the wonder of being "with" the God—the divine someone—became reality. The sense of belonging that I enjoyed with my parents before their grief returned to me, but this time it was bigger than all of us together.

The early fingerprints of wonder (divine curiosity and delight) and wound (brokenness and pain) circled throughout my life. Wonder looked like playing in the dirt in the front yard with a swiped kitchen spoon. It looked like being a valued and contributing family member "working" in my grandparent's deli. It looked like writing tales and drawing pictures on brown paper sacks. Wonder looked like reading the stories of Jesus in the Gospels and imagining myself in them. Meanwhile, my wounds looked like doing whatever it took to be accepted by friends or family. They looked like exchanging integrity for plasticity. I wasn't naughty enough for my peer group and wasn't good enough for the church group. Despite my constant compulsion to belong, I just didn't.

My wounds didn't have the final word, though. The Spirit who desired me into being wanted me to discover that my belonging was never in question. My good friend Juanita Rasmus, who is a spiritual director and contemplative teacher, walked with me through healing prayer. Together we tenderly entered my childhood memory and found that God was present in the pickup truck. Juanita's gentleness and full presence reflected God's, and I drank it in. Imagination in the tender hands of the Spirit helped me to feel the warmth of the sun as a blanket of God's love and protection. Even as my parents grieved, God was with me. In the aspens, God was with me. When I was begging for acceptance from my peers, God was with me. When I was trying and failing to be welcomed and honored as a girl with a gift to lead, God was with me. To live fully into my relationship with God required a look at my wounds, giving them the attention and care that wounds deserve.

DEATH COMES TO TEA

In February of 2011, my grandmother called to let me know that they were putting my grandfather in hospice care. He had been diagnosed with pancreatic cancer and there was nothing more to be done. He wanted to die at home, and my grandmother knew she couldn't take care of him all by herself. I loaded up my children and all our homeschooling stuff and traveled from Colorado to Texas to help. I learned that to be with another in their last days on this earth is a sacred task.

For nearly a month, I homeschooled the kids by day and cared for my grandfather by night. But mostly I was just company to my grandmother as she watched someone she loved for sixty-one years slip away. I wanted to be with her and my grandfather in this most tender part of their lives. The familiar fear around death was hard to ignore. It was present in the memory of my sister's death, and I watched it in the different responses of my family members.

Throughout the first half of my life, death had been like an unwelcomed acquaintance standing in the corner. I was always aware of its presence but tried not to look it in the face. But in the last month of my grandfather's life on this earth, death moved from the corner to the middle of the room. I saw the work of death in a human body, I saw the mark of death on the hearts of loved ones, and I saw that in the midst of it all, God was present. No one ever dies alone. God who is with us when we take our first breath does not abandon us at our final sigh.

In February of 2016, death pulled up a kitchen chair and asked for a sandwich. Just five months earlier, my aunt had been diagnosed with breast cancer. As the doctors looked at our shared family history, they noticed that her father, my grandfather, had died of pancreatic cancer while his mother, my great-grandmother, had died at the young age of thirty-eight of breast cancer. Louise Rutherford's death left three small children without a mother and a familial gash a mile deep and a mile wide.

The trend prompted the doctors to test my aunt for a range of genetic abnormalities that lead to breast cancer. Her test came back positive for the BRCA2 genetic abnormality. Those who have the BRCA2 abnormality lack a "kill switch" for certain cancer cells that develop into cancers of the breast, ovaries, prostate, pancreas, and potentially others. My aunt reached out in love to her family, urging us to get tested as well. That March the tests revealed that I, too, am positive for this genetic abnormality.

Over the next year deep questions around death and fear, the ones that had been rattling around in my mind and heart since my sister's death, came front and center. Could be they came at just the right time, as middle age has a way of dragging these up. In my praying and pondering, I returned to the places of wonder in my childhood, the places where I first sensed that I was not alone. I went outside. I walked and wandered all over our forty acres in western Colorado. I noticed the sharp substance of the prickly pear, the sacred gathering of scrub oak, and the mountain bluebirds.

For years I had been praying the *Divine Hours*, Phyllis Tickle's take on fixed-hour prayer throughout the day. The line from Psalm 103 came to mind: "For he knows how we were made; he remembers that we are dust." Wandering around outside, I came upon a shallow hole, a digging attempt by our border collies for comfort. Collies love to dig holes to curl up their bodies during winter for warmth and during the summer for cooling. They take advantage of the earth's gift of steady temperature. I lowered myself into one of these holes and rolled the Psalm around in my heart again.

> For he knows how we were made;
>> he remembers that we are dust.
> As for mortals, their days are like grass;
>> they flourish like a flower of the field;
> for the wind passes over it, and it is gone,
>> and its place knows it no more. (Psalm 103:14-16)

I took a deep breath and imagined my breath slowing, my heart stopping, and the life leaving my body. I let my body come to a complete rest in the dirt hole and imagined the decomposition processes beginning. I felt the weight of sadness and loss, a longing to see and hold my children, the smell of honeysuckle and sage, the sharp sting of a snowball perfectly aimed. These integral parts of incarnational, sensory living made me weep. A steady stream of tears flowed, welcomed by the earth as loss upon loss crashed into one another. This life, my life, was a wonder. But eventually, if Nature did her thing, there would be no trace of me left in this form. Every atom in my body would be dispersed elsewhere. Likely my family would tell a few "Lacy stories" (Lord have mercy, please choose the good ones), but after a generation or two even memories of me would be gone. For crying out loud, this life is so fleeting, so short. All was bittersweet: sorrow and sweetness, brokenness and beauty, longing and loss.

It is hard to put into words what happened as I lay in the dog hole with my body relaxed and my eyes closed. I do know that at one point all three of our dogs showed up and sat next to me, no doubt wondering what in the world I was doing in their hole. I had seen intimately what a death from pancreatic cancer looked like, and I didn't want it, but I wasn't afraid. I felt loss and sadness, but not one drop of fear. God was with me, and my belonging in God couldn't be unraveled, even as my body would surely return to dust. And there was something else: wonder woke up. Sorrow had caught deep in my gut for all that I would miss in the death of my life here on earth. But now it flowered into gratitude and wonder. The brevity of it all was like a sharp stick to the eye that helped me see more clearly.

The cool red Colorado clay supported and welcomed my body. I opened my eyes to see that I was surrounded by life. Faithful border collies attentive and protective, a cat wandering by passing judgment, little brown birds at the feeder, red ants, pill bugs, sage, pinyon pine, and wild rye welcomed me to this living school of wonder.

Oh! that there was a ground to lie in.

Oh! that these wooly and wonderful beasts might accompany me in life and in death.

Oh! that we created beings have a home that cannot be shaken.

Oh! that there was breath in my lungs, movement in my body.

The blue of the mountain bluebird was vibrant with joy. Oh yes! In this life we will have sorrow, and we will have wonder. In the withness of God and the withness of being part of the fabric of living, I found healing for my wounds and the raucous reawakening of wonder.

LIFE IS LIKE A SPIRAL (NOT LIKE A BOX OF CHOCOLATES, WHICH GRIEVES ME)

Westerners like me are a linear people. We appreciate a forward momentum that allows us to leave the past behind and focus on the future. Although following a recipe (that is, adhering to a linear process) might yield delicious brownies, life generally just doesn't work that way. A + B = C is great for algebra, but that's about it.

Our human journey is more like a spiral or Celtic knot. Imagine a spiral staircase that flows downward into increasingly tiny revolutions, the sides getting closer together with each turn, leading to unity with God. The shape of our human journey is something like this. We begin our life at the widest revolution of the spiral, living and learning from a place of wonder, discovery, and delight. We are fully present and connected to life. As infants and children, we are wired for connection. It's essential to our survival, so we make eye contact and we mirror the people surrounding us. We are also learning organisms, so every part of us is present to our surroundings, taking in information that shapes and forms us. We experience God this way too. With innocence, we encounter God through first-time engagement with this new world we live in. As we learn, our relationship with God takes shape too.

God, who is not bound by human developmental stages, longs to connect with us our whole life long. And so God does. Through loving adults, through experiences of goodness, beauty, truth, wonder, and more, we encounter and connect with God. We are rooted in humble innocence, born in and living from the generous heart of God. We are wondering participants in God's generous world. We begin in wonder.

As we walk the spiral of life, these experiences stay with us, sometimes as vivid memories, but more often as faint echoes of something we once knew. The wonder goes deep. Sometimes these memories are covered over by wounds, but they are not lost and they can be reclaimed.

And we are wounded. Our wounds and the wounds of the world run deep too. They drag us away from wonder and therefore away from connecting deeply with God and others. Our wounds deceive us about our fundamental identity as children of God. We expend energy, and a lot of it, trying to outrun our wounds or pretend they don't exist. Yet in our woundedness God is with us, still inviting us to connect, to lean in, and bring our woundedness into the light. Care for our wounds begins by admitting their presence, and then treating the infection they cause, assessing and addressing the damage. The historical church has dumped countless resources into wound management, to the exclusion of the early experience of wonder.[1] Reclaiming our early experiences of wonder will help to heal our wounds and lead us more deeply into the withness of God.

WANDERING IN WONDER

Eve and Adam lived who knows how long in peace, harmony, and joy with God. God fashioned them in God's own image and likeness. God, the Holy Knitter, wove creativity and agency, goodness, beauty, and truth right into their being. Our knitter knew that like winter clothes bought in summer, these new human beings would need to grow into the boots of beauty; they would need to grow into the trousers of truth. God is ever patient. He knew there would be time for that; they were eternal beings. Never one for missing a chance to celebrate, God threw a party on the sixth day complete with gifts. As told in Genesis 1:29-31, God, the purveyor of goodness and beauty, gave Eve and Adam handmade works of art: the earth and all that was in it. God and God's new friends partied so hard they had to rest on the seventh day.

On the second telling of the way of generosity (Genesis 2), God, the Cosmic Gardener, gets her hands dirty. God sinks hands in the newly created earth and lovingly forms and fashions. Then God breathes God's own breath into human lungs, implanting a longing for connection and intimacy. That longing, like a beacon, constantly reminded these humans that they were created for community. These humans were created by the Trinitarian Community of Love, and they would forever long for, strive for, seek, and search out connection. As Eve and Adam lived with God over the course of time, they grew in trust; they were surrounded by the way of generosity.

This is our first story. This is the generous way into which we were created. We are part of this glorious tapestry of love. All of humanity shares this story of belonging. As adults, our faithful work is to re-member it.

WALKING WITH WOUNDS

What begins in God-soaked wonder soon moves to human wounding. Human wounding starts early in life and leads to brokenness with others, with God, and within ourselves. Genesis chapter three narrates the story of this brokenness. While living in loving, generous community with God and each other, seeds of distrust are sown and brokenness begins. If Christian philosopher Dallas Willard is right and love is to will the very best good of another,[2] then at the heart of this brokenness are the questions, "Does God really have my best good in mind? Does God really love me?" The fault line of that break in relationship is distrust. Love and generosity shift to suspicion and scarcity.

Eve and Adam no longer knew what they thought they had known about God. Their experiential knowledge of God was forgotten, challenged, and ultimately suspect. One can hardly read the narrative of the first sin and not hear the echo of questioned love in Eve's heart when the serpent whispers, "Did God say . . . ?" (Genesis 3:1). What Eve and Adam believed about God was shaken—shaken even to the point of not trusting that God had their very best good in mind. Once that happened, all hell broke loose.

Along our human journey, just as with Eve and Adam, when our perceived needs are unmet and our sense of safety shaken, we slip into patterns of distrust and woundedness. We learn the way of scarcity. We are wounded and begin to wound others. In our woundedness we experience the way of scarcity and traverse its sparse peaks and death valleys. Over a lifetime, we develop survival skills to navigate a once-generous but newly disrupted and disintegrating world. We become compulsively attached, turning in on ourselves and harming others.

There are moments, though, when we hop back and forth between the generous and the scarce almost unnoticeably. Moments of unfathomable kindness, unconditional love, or unplanned goodness remind us that there is another way. As we navigate these hops, a longing stirs in us to be grounded in the generosity and wonder we once knew by heart.

We are jostled into an awareness that we don't have to live this way. We hear God's invitation to become more deeply connected. An intentional shift begins and we start to search for the generous way to which we belong. Maggie Ross puts it like this:

> Over time we become obliquely aware that something has shifted slightly, that something has been justified—not in the sense that we have proved right and everyone else wrong, but rather in the sense that all our fragments have become slightly better aligned, integrated, infused with the ineffable welcome we call *grace*.[3]

WRAPPED WITH GOD

Throughout our journey, God never abandons us. Instead God invites us on a circular learning path to deeper connection. The doubts that rattled around in Eve's heart are part of her deepening relationship with God. What is tried can be strengthened. What led her on the path of woundedness was blind self-sufficiency and fear. "You are alone; you can only depend upon yourself," came the voice from the shadows. Woundedness gripped her soul, and she acted on it. Through the pain and struggle of pregnancy, childbirth, and a longing for soul connection, she would learn. Bringing and building new life in this world would break her body and her heart. She would come to the end of herself and find God there. God would be with her in the blood, sweat, and tears as she brought new life into the world. God would be with her in the searing grief when one son murdered another. And God loved her like no person ever could. God was father, lover, protector, and friend.

But Adam needed a different school. He needed to learn to listen more deeply to his own longings at the cross section of where God's desires met his own. Through the pain and struggle of work he would grow a servant's heart, come to terms with his own finitude, and lay down the unbearable burden of emperorship. He would learn to connect deeply with others, setting his own needs aside. He too would come to the end of himself and find God there. God would be with him in the backbreaking—sometimes mind-numbing—work. God would be with him as he watched all that he'd worked for come to naught. God loved him like no person ever could. God was mother, lover, colaborer, and friend.

Compassionate correction is God's way. It shapes us, relying on our God-given predisposition to learn. And since we are a learning species, learning is always circular. What we learn at one level must permeate down to the deepest parts of who we are. And this takes time, sometimes thousands of years. Exodus 34 chronicles God's re-giving of the Ten Commandments, ultimately the gift of wisdom and guidance, to Moses and the people of Israel. In the giving, God reiterates his own character traits: compassion, mercy, slowness to anger, unfailing love, and forgiveness. God acknowledges that it could take a thousand generations for this to sink in.

God also acknowledges that the way of scarcity, the wounds of parents, children, and grandchildren, are also passed on to third and fourth generations. This we also learn.

When we have the courage to stay near to our pain rather than running from it, and to participate in the healing rather than re-wounding, restoration unfolds in the present and then flows to a thousand future generations—and even to past generations. Healing work is a must and a mystery. It is the economy of the kingdom of God; it is God's generosity at work (Exodus 20:1-6).

RE-MEMBERING

Forgetfulness is characteristic of our woundedness. There are over 150 references to the practice of remembering in the Bible, including to remember God's faithfulness, remember promises made, remember stories, and remember truths in danger of being lost. Therefore, much of our work requires remembering. Not only recalling, but literally re-membering: reattaching, integrating the parts of ourselves (our childhood selves) that have been buried, lost, ignored, or deliberately set aside. The movement from wounded to healing integration is about a life that is full to bursting with trust, hope, and love. It is a life mobilized by grace.

As we re-member, we learn to trust the Spirit to do the heavy lifting, just as children learn. We develop wider wisdom, greater character, and deeper love for God, self, and others. The longings and lessons learned through wonder and wound guide us back to God's generous way that we knew in our beginnings. This journey will transform us. While we may not regain our childhood innocence, we will gain a Christlike character. We grow into God's adult children.

God's generosity means that there is no waste in the spiritual life. There are no throwaway events or people—much as we might chafe against that idea. Every experience, be it good or ill, can be used for God's glory and our very best good. In a linear framework there is waste, that which doesn't fit the prescribed path. But in a circular framework everything can be used. We only need to go outside and read nature, the first revelation of God, to see that everything belongs. Everything is useful.

Welcoming Practices

Create an altar. Find a space where you can create a small altar reminding you of God's generous way and your identity as beloved of God. Place pictures of yourself as a child on your altar. You might also include a candle, a passage of Scripture, or a poem that speaks to you of God's generous way. Keep it simple and meaningful. Less is more when it comes to altars. Visit this space once a day for at least five minutes. Allow yourself to bask in God's love for you.

Reflect on your life thus far. Notice the threads of both wonder and wounding. What stories do you tell around these themes in your life? Create a collage using magazine clippings or other images that show the interwoven nature of these threads. Is there one thread that could use more attention? The children's picture book *Perfect Square* by Michael Hall can help to enliven your imagination for the process of reconstruction and redemption.

Learn through a book. Read and reread the children's picture book *When God Made You* by Matthew Paul Turner and David Catrow. Notice the invitation to wonder about your own early life with God. When you find yourself overwhelmed, read Ruth Goring's *Isaiah and the Worry Pack*. What conversations with Jesus arise in you?

3

Reattaching to Our Divine Parent

*Jesus' identity is inseparable from his being
a child in the bosom of the Father.*

HANS URS VON BALTHASAR

I was nine months pregnant. It was July and I was standing in
line with my three-year-old, Aidan, at "the Walmart."

If that's not enough to garner an empathetic response, you are
either dead or have never been to Walmart. I was far too large and
it was far too hot to be wearing any clothing, but in the interest of
the delicate sensibilities of my rural Colorado neighbors, I'd
opted for something like a tent. Unfortunately, even the tent was
too small.

We were out of toilet paper, and someone had to strike out
in search of some. So I had put on the tent and my underwear
with the least-binding elastic. Standing in line, I was slung over
one end of the cart like a soggy dishrag while my three-year-old

delivered her best gymnastics routine on the other, complete with onlookers and cheers. At the very least, it lightened the somber mood that hot July day. After a while, we inched our way to the cashier and began to exchange a few pleasantries.

"Yes, it is hot." "Yes, I am pregnant." "No, I don't think it would be funny if my water broke." For crying out loud, people, do you want me to cry in public again?

Out of the corner of my eye, I saw a man walking toward us. Aidan was frightened. She stopped right in the middle of her half twist at the end of the cart, crawled through the spot for dog food, and right up my tent. The garment was not really big enough for the two of us—me and the baby—and it certainly wasn't big enough for the three of us.

My long-overstretched underwear abandoned its post. I tried my own gymnastic move to keep it from falling on the floor, and Aidan helped by wrapping her arms around my legs so tight it could only land on the top of her head. The lady behind me grabbed the hem of my tent and tried to tug it over the three of us—a futile effort something akin to helping a hippo get into a cheerleading skirt. If it is true that every day we need a dose of humiliation to continue to grow in our life with God, I'm set for a while. All full here.

As I retold that story to the uproarious laughter of my family, I noticed something about our Walmart adventure. When Aidan was afraid, she ran to me, her mother, her protector, the one she trusts, the one she knows loves her. At three years old, she didn't have a cache of intellectual knowledge, and she didn't need to reason out her options; she just bolted to me and got as close as possible. We've had some history together. In fact, from her point of view, all of her history has been within my protection. I am safe and I can create safety for her. I have fed her when she was hungry. I have comforted her when she was hurt. I have protected her from perceived threats. On that boiling July day, she trusted her own instincts, acknowledged her fear, and ran to the safety of her mother.

As I reflected, I realized that I don't often run to God when I am afraid. With my words I say that God is "a very present help in trouble" (Psalm 46:1), but my actions communicate something else. There are times when I can't even acknowledge that I am afraid. I not only run from God, I also run from fear.

When securely attached children are anxious, worried, or afraid, they reach for the safest person they know and trust. Connection cultivates trust in children. It is beyond their rational consideration; it is a hidden knowledge that reverberates throughout the dimensions of their person. It is in their bodies, it is in their feeling centers, and it is mystery. When we adults experience intense fear, we fight, flee, freeze, or *tend and befriend*. Most of us know what fight, flight, or freeze looks like, but that last one might be new. To tend and befriend is a response to fear when we sense that we are powerless.[1] We use what we've got to make the threat see us as an ally and a support, even when we know they are set on our destruction.

When our fear is triggered, our defenses are thrown into high gear. We activate the systems of scarcity and run away, fight off the intruder, or cower as we try to make ourselves smaller and less threatening, inching ever closer to our own disappearance. So what about you? When you are afraid, what do you do? Where do you turn?

STAGES OF ATTACHMENT

The stories that we tell ourselves about the past shape the life we are living in the present. To be sure, we are not reliving factual accounts of events in our history. Instead, we are reliving the *meanings* we've made of these stories. These stories and the meanings we make matter. They form the way we see and experience the world, ourselves, and even God.

Canadian developmental psychologist Gordon Neufeld outlined six stages of attachment to explain the development of attachment in children.[2] These six stages are: proximity, sameness, belonging or loyalty, significance, love, and being known.

The stages are present in adult and divine attachment too. As we grow in our life with God, we pass through these stages over and over again, each at a deeper level. First, in order to attach to our Divine Parent, we must experience God near to us. Attachment happens as we share experiences in our daily lives with God, as we see God's movement and notice God's responsiveness to us as precious children.

Next, we also must see ourselves reflected in God—the divine other. At some point we must experience ourselves as having the divine spark. We see this clearly in God's creation of us. Since God made us in God's image and likeness, we share a level of "sameness" that produces a deeply connective attachment.

Neufeld names the third stage "belonging" or "loyalty." In our deep attachment with God, we must have an experiential knowledge of acceptance and place, held and welcomed by the benevolent Creator of life and light.

The fourth stage, significance, flows from our sense of belonging and not the other way around. We learn that God is actively for us.

Seeking our significance before settling into our belonging leads to a life of chasing after our identity and an insatiable attachment to work and achievement in order to gain that identity.[3] Life-giving attachment to our Divine Parent is not built on our behavior, but God's love and commitment to us as their child. We move into the fifth attachment stage of a shared love that is lasting.

Once we have moved through these five stages, we are sufficiently attached to share our deepest thoughts, feelings, and even the most wounded parts of who we are. In being known, we reach the sixth and final stage of one level and can begin again at a deeper level of who we are and who God is. Passing through these stages and levels of attachment roots us more deeply into the mystery of our eternal life with God.

There are many bumps and setbacks along the way. For some of us, those early stories that we continue to live through are not ones that lead to attachment. In these lived stories, we may not have developed a deep trust in the adults in our lives, and therefore didn't develop a deep trust in God. And particular misguided teachings of the early stories in the Bible may have led us to feel that God is not for us, much less loving.

In his book *Not in God's Name: Confronting Religious Violence*, Rabbi Jonathan Sacks opens the reader to deeper meanings woven throughout the first stories of the patriarchs found in Genesis and Exodus. Using linguistic and cultural clues combined with the Jewish gift of midrash, we can see a new story unfolding:

> Beneath the surface, in a series of counter-narratives, it tells the opposite story, subverting the whole frame of mind that says, "Either you or me. If you win, I lose. If I win, you lose." That may be true of scarce goods like wealth or power. It is

not true of divine love, which is governed by the principle of plenitude.[4]

This principle of plenitude shapes what we believe about God and how, or if, we move through the stages of attachment.

YOUR EARLY STORY

Let's start with a practice to orient us. Find a nice quiet spot out of the reach of sound (TV, music, people talking). Parents of children, feel free to hide in the pantry or bathroom—no parental guilt here if you need to turn on a cartoon babysitter for a bit. Now, find a blank piece of paper. Any kind of paper will work; feel free to use the back of an envelope or a lost-and-now-found permission slip. (I would say toilet paper, but in my experience, it is too valuable for the survival of a functional family and therefore should not be sacrificed.) You will also need a writing utensil: crayon, pen, pencil, charcoal, whatever.

Next: get comfortable. I know it's difficult in a small pantry that smells of Cheerios and boxed wine, but you can do it. Close your eyes and rummage around in your mind for a picture of yourself when you were three, four, or five years old. Hold that picture lovingly. Notice that kid.

For just a minute, take a long loving look at that little one. Muster up as much love and compassion as you can for your young self. Think back as far as you can and recall an early encounter with God. If you don't have that memory, try to remember when you first heard about God, or remember an early thought you had about God. Give yourself a generous amount of time to wander around in that memory. Now, place your chosen writing utensil in your nondominant hand and draw your memory.

Take your time and get all the details you can remember on the paper. Don't worry about the quality of your drawing. It doesn't need to look like a Rembrandt, or, for that matter, look like anything. You're not going to enter this into the county art show and, for crying out loud, you're in the pantry—the Cheerios don't care. When you've finished, look at your drawing. See it as you would see a drawing that a beloved child offered to you. Have at least as much compassion for yourself as you would have for a beloved child.

Enter into a conversation with God about your drawing. What is actually there? What is delightful? What is painful? What *isn't* there? Notice your strongest emotions and bring them into your conversation. Tell God about this drawing and then listen to what God has to say. God can speak through a word or phrase, an image, a feeling, a recalled portion of Scripture, or song. Be open to impressions that might surface.

I have led adults in this exercise many times, and each time folks have been surprised at what they discover. For some, this exercise unlocks a memory they hadn't thought of in years: a stroll in the trees at a young age when they suddenly knew that God was with them, or a time when they heard their mother praying and God answered. Perhaps it was a time when they just knew in the smile of their grandmother or a kind Sunday school teacher that God was good. Maybe it was the felt nearness of God at the death of a pet or a question of meaning or existence that came up while they were playing in the ocean.

But for some of us this exercise unlocks a memory that reflects nothing of the character of God found in Jesus. An abusive father, a harsh or judgmental experience at church, separation from loved ones, or childhood trauma all can be part of our early memories associated with God. Whatever your experience may be, can I take you up and out of your feelings and into your rational thinking for a moment?

CHECK YOUR IMAGE

Check your embedded memory against 1 Corinthians 13, which sketches the character of God.

God is love, and therefore God is patient. God is kind. God is not envious or boastful or arrogant or rude. God will not insist on God's own way; God is not irritable or resentful. God does not rejoice in wrongdoing but rejoices in the truth. God bears all things, believes all things, hopes all things, endures all things. God and God's love for you will never end.

Does your memory reflect God's character?

If it does, savor it like you would your favorite dessert. Roll it around in your active memory and let every moment dissolve into celebrated bliss. Does it have a color, a shape, a smell? As I mentioned previously, my early memory of meeting God was in a grove of aspen trees. It was wet, spongy, and had a distinctly fresh smell. I have drawn that scene (poorly, mind you) hundreds of times over the years. I have taken hiking trips into groves of these trees to re-member, literally reattaching this memory to my picture of God.

If your memory does not match with the character of God found in 1 Corinthians 13, please know that while this is an early memory, this isn't the whole story. Before and during this wounding, the Spirit was reaching toward you; the Spirit was surrounding you with goodness, truth, and beauty. Even this difficult memory is not without God's presence. Bring it to God in prayer and discuss it with your spiritual director or trusted friend. Painful memories begin to lose their power over us when we bring them to the light. Other early encounters with God may have not gotten much memory traction, but they are not completely lost. Like me, you can locate and re-member.

Asking is a superpower of the kingdom of God. Feel free to use it; ask God to bring a memory to mind. Be patient and listen to your dreams and other moments of your current life that might resonate. Feel free to also use a current memory. Has someone loved you well in the last few years? What is life giving to you, and how might that reflect God's love for you? Letting the Spirit repair trust can take time. Be gentle with your precious self. Go slow and count the goods as they come.

In their extensive research on children's spirituality, Robert Coles, Rebecca Nye, and David Hay came to the conclusion that children have early experiences of God.[5] When you were a child, you had experiences of God. Remember that the first stage of attachment is proximity. As God designed the system, God has scattered God's self throughout the world. God has always been near. But as a child you might not have labeled your experiences as God, or even registered them as significant. Making meaning of an event helps it to stick in our memories. So, if we didn't make meaning of an event at the time, it might not have stuck; but it did happen.

Being in God's wonder-filled presence is a child's natural state, not an anomaly. Anomalies give our memories traction, but daily life, not so much.

If there was one significant adult in your life with whom you shared your experience, and if that adult acknowledged that your experience was valid and encouraged your continued engagement with God, you formed a lasting, functional memory. That adult helped you make meaning. If you didn't have this kind of listening and encouragement, your experience was likely buried under other louder memories. Our God experiences aren't just a one-off; each young life is surrounded with and woven through with these experiences.

As Sacks says, "divine love . . . is governed by . . . plenitude."[6] It is characteristic of God's generous way to lavish children with his presence. The Spirit has been reaching for you since your beginning. You were born into the way of generosity, but somewhere that memory may have been forgotten. However, all is not lost. The Holy Knitter wove those memories into your mind and heart, and they can be found and flagged.

Researchers from the Religious Education Research Centre in Wales asked adults about their childhood experiences of God and then organized the results in categories such as wonder, mystery, awe, nature, woven threads of meaning, tears, and unity.[7] Let's unpack these just a bit.

Goodness is whatever leads to human flourishing. Do you have a memory of experienced goodness when you were a child?

Beauty is goodness made alive to the senses, says Christian philosopher Dallas Willard.[8] Can you remember an experience of something that captured your senses?

Truth is an experience that reverberates deep within us. Truth has the ring of the real and authentic. It has a longevity that holds through tests and trials. When you rummage around in your memory, what has held? Is there a thought, idea, understanding that has had staying power, even today?

Wonder is a divinely given curiosity that grows as we notice the world around us. Through wonder, we gladly give mental space to the unfolding of human awareness. How did you wonder about the world as a child?

Mystery is a grateful resignation to what we don't know. There is no conscious resignation to live in mystery for children; they live there quite naturally. They know that they don't know, and that knowledge frees them up to a transcendent experience of what is before them. When as a child did you feel free to not know?

Awe is a full-bodied reverential experience of our core connection to all of creation. Awe will unconsciously cause our whole bodies to expand as we try to take it all in. Was there a time in your childhood when you experienced awe?

Nature is the first revelation of God. It is a place that goodness, beauty, and truth are most vivid and alive. What is it like to remember being outside as a child?

Woven threads of meaning are when things fit together in unmistakable ways, helping us to make meaning. Was there a time when, like puzzle pieces fitting together, you noticed that events or experiences fit together, and it helped you make sense of something?

Tears heighten our awareness of our longing for God, especially when we are children. Our patterns for hiding pain haven't quite become habitual, so we are more tender to God's loving presence and our desire for love. Was there a time when pain or loss heightened your sense of God's presence or your own tender longing for God?

Unity is an experience of connection so deep that our self-preoccupation thins or disappears all together. Can you remember a time when you lost track of time or when you felt so close to another living being that you forgot about yourself?

The following exercise is best practiced with a conversational partner. Tell about an early memory of goodness—something really good that happened when you were a child. Tell about your first memory of beauty; think back to something that caught your attention and kept it. Tell your story about a truly wonder-filled experience. Take time with each of these categories and search your memories for God's presence. In a newsletter titled *Apocalyptic Hope,* Father Richard Rohr tells a story about the lights on his family's Christmas tree capturing his sense of wonder.[9] It can be something as simple as that.

Likely one story will lead to another. Once you begin to open up these stories, your memory will give you a few more. Tell a story about something that struck you as funny or something that sparked your curiosity. You may even dream about some of your childhood stories. If you do, be sure to write them down as soon as you wake up. Feelings are our first line of awareness, so it can be helpful to first capture your strongest feeling in the first waking moment. Then progress to writing out as many of the details as you can remember.

Telling these stories can help us escape from the way of scarcity. In his powerful book *Jesus and the Disinherited,* Howard Thurman offers guidance to those who have been and continue to be under the yoke of injustice. For people whose "backs are up against the wall," he calls out three "hounds of hell": fear, deception, and hate.[10] When we are living in the way of scarcity—whether chosen or forced on us—these hounds police the border, making sure we never even think about going home to the generous way.

Fear is the first hound, and it begins to stalk us early in our lives. Thurman advises that fear can only be vanquished by an experiential knowledge of ourselves as God's beloved. We can strengthen our attachment to the generous and good God of the first stories in Genesis. We re-member what we innately knew about God when we were children. Rummaging through our early memories and savoring experiences of wonder, mystery, awe, tears, nature, woven threads of meaning, and unity help us to reattach to our Mothering Father.

The second hound Thurman names is *deception*. Fear feeds on duplicity, delusion, and denial. Pretending that we are not afraid and distracting ourselves from facing our fear only prolongs the suffering. As adults, we tell stories that aren't true in order to get away from the truth that our fear embodies. But we need to be like young children, who are present to their fear in the most vulnerable way. They have not yet developed defenses against their fear and cannot help but be fully present to it. Vulnerability in the presence of a loving adult drains the power from fear. Admitting our fear and confessing our weakness shortens the distances between us, God, and others.

Hate is the third hound Thurman named. For some of us, our childhood selves and the memories associated with those years rouse feelings of disgust and even hate. We may have experienced abuse, trauma, or shame at the hands of those who held power. Perhaps your memory is a story that family or friends tell that makes you cringe and brings you shame. The danger with disgust or hating our childhood selves is that, as Thurman writes, "Hatred cannot be controlled once it is set in motion." The hate that we might feel for our childhood or adolescent selves is still with us and it guides how we view ourselves now, how we see others, and how we experience God.

But Thurman doesn't leave us with hate. He reminds us that love is our mandate. We are members of love's family: love is our home. We can learn to love our childhood selves by beginning to reestablish our relationship with ourselves. In the re-membering of our early encounters with God, we allow the Spirit to make meaning for us. We lend understanding to our childhood selves, and in that understanding, we become free of shame and bitterness.

Our journey began with wonder, moved through wound, and now invites us into withness. Surrounded by God's generous way, we can welcome and be with our childhood selves.

RE-MEMBERING THE GOOD SHEPHERD

Within six weeks of finding out that I was positive for the BRCA2 genetic abnormality, I had a prophylactic double mastectomy and my ovaries removed. Hello, old body issues and hot flashes capable of melting my mettle.

In the weeks leading up to the surgical removal of my breasts and ovaries, old fears came knocking and brought new friends. There hadn't been a time since my teens when I loved my body. The old taunts of high school boys joined with my own disdain. In this scarce land where my very genetics seemed hell bent on killing me, I came face-to-face with fear. I looked at my daughters in their early teen years and feared for them. Would they too have to go through this? Would I live to see them go to college? I was forty-five; I had beaten my great-grandmother by four years. Was I on borrowed time?

The Spirit often shows up like a cool, soft wind on a hot, airless day. Several years earlier, I had the incredible opportunity to earn seminary credit at the Renovaré Institute. It is a two-year program of spiritual formation in the way of Jesus. Early on, we were directed to memorize Psalm 23, the Good Shepherd psalm. I spent a month in this psalm, wallowing it into my active memory, noting times in my early life where this good, generous, protective Shepherd surrounded me with love and care.

Up until the day of the mastectomy, fear was my go-to emotion. Tightness in my jaw, neck, and shoulders; nausea, and a racing heart were common in the weeks leading up to it. I distracted myself by marathon-watching old episodes of *Friends*. Hilarious, but not my smartest move. I worried how my body would look and feel after the surgeries. I worried about pain and, curiously enough, how my shirts would fit.

Dr. Anne was my surgeon. She was kind, tender, and reassuring. She even comforted and hugged my mother, saying, "I promise I will take care of her." It was one of the most beautiful scenes I have witnessed. And she's an excellent surgeon. I decided against reconstruction and went, as we call it in the mastectomy world, "flat and fabulous." I couldn't be more pleased with the outcome. (Choosing to go flat or reconstructed is an intimately private choice, and both can be paths leading to healing and wholeness.)

Just before being wheeled into the operating room, Dr. Anne asked me to raise my body to a sitting position. She needed to make a few marks on my breasts with what looked like purple marker. I assumed they were guides for incisions. I gripped the cold steel railing of the hospital bed to pull myself into a sitting position. She gently opened the front of my hospital gown and I watched her make the purple marks that would lead to a dramatic reduction of my risk of breast cancer, and ultimately invite me to a re-membering of my body, a childlike acceptance of my physical presence. The reality of what was about to happen flooded my eyes, my brain and my body began to shake. Summoning all my courage to hold still, I heaved a huge sigh that ruffled the hospital gown ties. At the moment of my exhalation the Spirit whispered the wallowed words and images of Psalm 23.[11]

I am your shepherd,

I give you everything that you need.

I bring you to good places where there is plenty to eat
and drink;

I give you the kind of rest that restores and re-members
your soul.

I guide you to paths of health and wholeness

Because that is who I AM.

Even as you walk through the valley of the shadow of death,

Fear no evil, for I AM with you.

I protect you.

I am so generous and good that there is enough for all
of humanity.

My love for each of you never ceases.

There is more than enough.

Goodness and mercy shall follow you all the days of
your life;

We are together forever. You are never alone.

My lips remembered the shape of the words and I began to say them aloud. Pictures of God's generosity that I had committed to sensory memory came one after another: the aspen groves of my childhood, the lap of an adult who loved me, the Oregon coast, the quiet presence of the kind-eyed quarter horse Pepper, my children moving in my womb, my mother's laugh. My body stopped shaking and a forgotten shalom spread, beginning in my chest and radiating down through my core and into my arms and legs. It was familiar. I knew this safe place. A hospital tech came to my bedside and asked if I was ready. "Yes," I answered, "I am ready."

Welcoming Practices

Picture yourself. Look through old pictures and find one or two of yourself when you were a young child. Begin by asking the Spirit to bring back to your mind experiences of goodness, beauty, truth, wonder, mystery, awe, nature, woven threads of meaning, tears, and unity.

Notice when you are afraid. Do you fight, flee, or freeze? Do you become defensive, run away, or do nothing? Or do you tend and befriend? Do you try to make everyone happy, comfy, and placated? When you begin to move into one of these habitual patterns, take a moment to stop and reflect. Tune into what you are doing and why you are doing it. Center yourself in God's generous, loving presence. Name this fear and bring it to God.

Learn from a book. Read the children's book *Making Heart-Bread* by Matthew Linn, Sheila Fabricant Linn, Dennis Linn, and Francisco Miranda. Practice "making heart-bread." Notice the presence of our Mothering Father throughout your day.

4

All God's Children Got Bodies

It takes enormous trust and courage
to allow yourself to remember.

BESSEL A. VAN DER KOLK

The shocking reality that the infinite God took on finite flesh comes to us each year at Christmas. Those with even a bit of theological education call this the incarnation. Simply put, this term means: God got a body. (And so much more, but work with me here.)

The incarnation is a distinctive tenet of our Christian faith. *Merriam-Webster* reminds us that to *incarnate* means to invest with human nature and form, to manifest or make comprehensible.[1] Matthew's Gospel, describing the angel's message for Mary and Joseph, clearly calls listeners to realities known to the prophet Isaiah: "'They shall name him Emmanuel,' which means, 'God is with us'" (Matthew 1:23). The Israelites learned over time that God was indeed with them as Spirit, but it was a different dance altogether for God to be with them in the flesh. If Dallas Willard was right in chapter eight of *Renovation of the Heart* that "spiritual formation requires the transformation of the body," we've got some work to do.[2]

And that work starts with welcome. Christianity is not a disembodied, esoteric religion of rejecting our bodies. We are human: flesh, dust from dust. Our bodies were created good. But take a little gander through our history, and we see that we've struggled to see the goodness of bodies. Many of us hold a disdain for our bodies, whether because of what we've been taught about our bodies or because of the way we've used them. Our culture hasn't been much help, either, and neither has the "gospel of sin management," a phrase that Willard uses to describe an unhealthy attachment to behavior management rather than whole-life transformation.[3] We have become adversaries of the unique, sacred bodies God gave us.

BEHOLDING OUR BODIES

To welcome our bodies in our spiritual formation, we behold. Beholding our bodies is an honoring act, something that our parents may have done upon our birth. God is continually beholding you, holding you and your body in a loving gaze every moment of your life. If you have ever held a beloved one (like a new baby), you know the soft glow of a sacred body. Take a moment and look at yourself in the mirror. You, your body is hallowed. No matter what has happened to it, no matter what you have done or left undone, the holy of your body cannot be erased. Our sacred bodies are created to reflect and radiate the sacred glow of God. This is not about worshiping bodies, which is a distortion. This is about honoring the glow of wonder which has been lovingly woven throughout. The Spirit began knitting us together in our mother's womb and continues the knitting today. Our bodies require no more than glory and no less.

We act on this beholding by *inhabiting* our bodies rather than *using* them. This requires us to learn to listen to our bodies. Instead of succumbing to habitual patterns woven within our bodies, what would it look like to program pauses throughout our days to listen to our bodies? What does our body tell us when we are in heated debates with loved ones? What does our body tell us when we seek comfort, distraction, or destruction?

If we listen to our bodies, we will hear of the wounds that they carry. Our bodies hold our wounds so that the mind and heart can get on with life. But bodies can only hold woundedness for so long before they require the tender attention of Jesus. If we are to train our bodies to uncover their God-given glory, we will need to cultivate compassion and let Jesus do the thing Jesus does best: heal our hurts.

BODIES BELONG

In Dallas Willard's anthropology of the person, bodies belong. Willard locates bodies as one dimension of the person. Note that they're just one dimension, and not at the center. While our bodies are important, they aren't all we are, and disaster strikes when our bodies are in charge. For Willard, the body is one of four key interdependent dimensions of the human person: alongside the body are the human spirit (also called the heart), mind (thoughts and feelings), and social context. Each dimension belongs to the others. Our bodies encapsulate an integration that transcends the toxic individuality of our time.

We belong—our bodies belong—to our social context. We belong to each other, as the principle of Ubuntu (meaning "I am because we are") from our South African sisters and brothers reminds us.[4] We belong to place, as we learn from our Indigenous sisters and brothers.[5] Ultimately our belonging is with God, the One who longed and loved us into being in the first place. Here, where human spirit touches Holy Spirit is the center of the person.

A STORY ABOUT A BODY

I was barely twenty-three, newly married and learning to live in a new city. Rochester, New York, was far away from where I had grown up in Texas, Colorado, and Utah. With more innocence and ignorance than education or wisdom, I landed my first teaching job at a little charismatic Christian school in the suburb of Penfield. I taught there for three years, beginning with seventh- and eighth-grade special education and then moving on to a fourth-grade class whose fingerprints I can still feel in my heart (and see on my social media feed). The charismatic community of beloveds was foreign to me at best, frightening at worst.

In my childhood, worship had looked like singing hymns to the back of each other's heads. Other than lips singing, and vocal cords engaged, there was to be no other movement, not even kneeling. (This surely was not the experience of every person present, but it was mine.) My first chapel experience at Penfield's New Covenant Christian School came just a year after the Toronto Blessing had upturned this part of the Christian world.

The Toronto Blessing was an embodied mystical experience of divine ecstasy. It began in a church in Toronto, Canada, which is just across Lake Ontario as the Spirit flies. People were overcome by divine love. They spoke in unrecognizable utterances, laughed uncontrollably, danced, and reported deep and inexplicable emotional healing. Manifestation of divine love spread from one church to others in this region.

When I came to Rochester, this kind of engagement with God was far outside my experiential knowledge for adults, but even more for children. Children, I had been taught in my childhood church, were separated from God until they reached an age where their reasoning capabilities could usher them into God's presence through confession. That, however, was not the living belief of Toronto's little group of merry fools. They believed that how God chooses to engage with us is up to God.

On the very first Wednesday, I brought my class into what looked like a gym that had been converted into a theater. A large stage with heavy curtains filled one entire side. We found our row and dutifully took our seats. On the stage, students and adults warmed up their instruments. The mother of one of my students plugged in her bass guitar and waved at her son, who was sitting next to me. A diverse swath of people held the stage: African American, Puerto Rican, Asian, Caucasian, Jewish, both young and old. Then, in a warm and rhythmic voice the music teacher, Mrs. Paris, bellowed the call, "Let's worship, church!" The children leaped to their feet and moved out into the aisles. I wondered if I had missed the fire drill alarm. Confused, I asked myself if it was my job to follow my class into the mob of students and "monitor" them. The thought was laughable really, as it wasn't even possible.

These children—who, just moments before, had been wrestling with long division, some with delight and some with dread—were now singing and dancing from a place of total freedom. They swayed, hopped, and skipped to the rhythm of the music; they raised their arms high in playful abandon with the God who longed them into being.

One of my students, Eric, a tall, gangly, African American child, came back for me. "Miss, you can come too. Worship is for everybody!"

I smiled at his generous invitation. "Maybe next time. I'll stay here today."

He shrugged his shoulders and went back in the midst of the other children, far freer than me to dance with the Spirit.

With each chorus that passed, my body stiffened. I stood as still as I could, battling old wounds. This buried my longing to allow my head to descend into my heart and come to full expression through my body. "Worship is for everybody," he had said. I wondered if he could be right, and I felt instantly jealous of the freedom he had to inhabit his body. I sang the words that stirred my feelings, but there was something in the flow of worship that compelled me to shut down.

Worship, like so many other things, is not linear. Rather, it is a circular flow where God and human come together in a playful way to honor and celebrate, with all the fullness of human beingness, the beingness of God. We can learn from our Eastern Orthodox sisters and brothers, who bow and kiss and make the sign of the cross in their embodied worship. They have known for more than two thousand years that worship needs a bodily expression.

In her book *Wisdom of the Body,* author and retreat leader Christine Valters Paintner compares the body to the wilderness, the place at the edge, where the ancient desert mothers and fathers went longing for an experience of God.[6] They were seeking a way of knowing in which God wasn't relegated to the political and religious elite. They were hungry for an experience of God that was as expansive as the desert landscape itself. Worship can stir up our hunger for the place at the edge. We might long to connect with God in ways that include our bodies; but like the desert, there is so much unseen, so much that lies outside conscious awareness, that we can mistrust the very bodies we live in.

We modern human beings are fascinated and fearful of what our bodies know. Our bodies hold our histories; they hold both the wonder and wound of our childhood selves. What a grace it is that our bodies will hold the glory and the gruesome for our collected selves so that we can go on with our living. However, like all dimensions of the human person, our bodies are limited. Our precious flesh and bone can only hold so much for so long without needing gentle attention. Anxiety and exhaustion build exponentially in our bodies as they hold the pain, grief, and sufferings of a life lived.

My female body held wounds that, while unaddressed, stopped the flow of worship. I could sing and I could feel the feelings in my heart, but I forced the worship to stop at my body.

Back at New Covenant Christian School, after a staff meeting, I had a confusing conversation with Mr. Rosenblum, who gave music lessons. He played his oboe during Wednesday worship and happened to have it with him.

"I notice you don't dance," he said as we walked down the hallway together.

"Well, yeah, I've never danced in worship before," I responded, a little embarrassed.

He stuck the reed of his oboe in his mouth and played a melody I could only identify as sounding *Jewish-like.* "Where do you feel this sound in your body?"

"My body?" I wondered, aloud.

"Yes, what part of your body wants to join the music?"

"I don't know. I'll have to think about it," I said, smiling quickly and then turning into my classroom. My body didn't want to join the music; it wanted to run.

For the next few weeks, I held forcibly still during chapel, and I listened for his oboe. The haunting music felt like joy and sorrow intermingling. I wondered which part of my body felt that kind of joy and sorrow, what part of my body needed that song. As I talked with God about the jealousy I felt for the children's freedom, something was shifting inside.

My hips are wide. Even when I was a teen and skinny as a rail, my hips were . . . let's just say "substantial." My grandmother used to say, "Your wide hips mean that you'll have babies easily." (What a liar she turned out to be.) For many women, their hips ground them in the moment, in their bodies, in their souls. Women, generally, hold power in the lower body. Quads carry us and the children we bear. Hips are made to hold—children and hands, both ours and those we allow. When women are feeling our worth, we shake our hips. Men, however, are grounded often through their shoulders; it is their power center where they hold the weight of their world.

During chapel, my shoulders were not in touch with the music, but my hips were. I don't know what shifted in me on that day. I can't say what broke loose. Certainly, there was a surrender of the fear of looking stupid, or childish, or simply crazy. But what began with a gentle sway, likely imperceivable to others, blossomed into full-bodied dancing with the children, singing with all my heart, soul, mind, and body. Eric gave me a high five while singing "Shine, Jesus, Shine." "Miss, you're here!" he shouted.

"Glad you worshiped with us today," Mr. Rosenblum said as I walked the children back to our classroom. "Are you Jewish? I think you might be Jewish." He spoke with all the seriousness of finding a long-lost relative.

"I don't think so—I'm from Texas," I answered. Then I disappeared with the children into our classroom.

This question would be asked again of me nearly twenty years later. "Are you Ashkenazi Jewish?" was the fifth question on the form I had to fill out to be tested for the BRCA2 mutation. To my knowledge I had no Jewish lineage. I checked the box labeled "no" and handed my form to the nurse. When my test came back positive, it stirred a curiosity in me around my heritage, since BRCA mutations are particularly high in Ashkenazi Jewish women (one in forty Ashkenazi Jewish women have the mutation).[7] I coughed up the cash and some spit and sent my sample to a genetic ancestry site and found out that 3 percent Ashkenazi is enough to inherit the genetic mutation. Mr. Rosenblum's intuition was a tiny bit right: I was, at least genetically, a little Jewish.

A BROKEN BODY

My friend Julie is a lawyer and a judge. She is the kind of friend who will come visit you in prison (but definitely won't help you hide a body). Not long after my prophylactic double mastectomy, she invited me to come to Zumba class with her. I hoped that dancing to Latin music would help to reduce my protruding belly, which many women notice after having a mastectomy without reconstruction. It was a shock to realize how much belly had been hiding under my boobs. Re-membering my body meant not only physical pain, but emotional pain. I had spent a good forty years trying to forget the shame my body held. Dance, I thought, might help.

One would think that the thump-thump of Latin beats would be enough to draw me in, but within the first few minutes, my resistance was even louder than the music. Simultaneously, two memories flashed through my mind, and I left the room. There was a running track outside, a space that was a little wider, a little quieter, where I could walk out my wounds.

"What do you shake when you've got no breasts?" This was just one of the questions I was living. What does gender, self-perception, and even self-acceptance look like after a mastectomy? The concern might seem silly, but in a room full of women who are shaking what they've got, I didn't know what to do when what I'd got was gone. The familiar feeling of shame flooded my mind and my body. It pulled me back to a memory from my adolescence.

Could anything make sitting in a high school health class, listening to sex education talks, more embarrassing? Yes, actually: sitting in front of oversexed, undermatured boys of privilege in a school that worshiped their existence. This was the school of *Friday Night Lights*, where boys were valued for their football skills and girls were valued by their ability to please the boys. Being a late bloomer put a target on my front. For weeks these boys assaulted me with questions about the state of my body. I tried to ignore them. I even tried to laugh with them. On better occasions, they spoke just loud enough for me to hear while sitting in front of them. On worse occasions they asked their taunting questions directly as I walked in the room. I felt ashamed that I seemed to always be a day late and a dollar short, even when it came to puberty. It was true, I wanted them to like me, to notice me, but not like this. Rather than becoming angry with them, I became angry with myself. Oh, why couldn't my body be pleasing? The root of shame twisted around my sense of self and cemented their damaging assessment.[8]

In his book *Walking in Wonder*, John O'Donohue writes, "The body is not an object to think about. Rather it is a grouping of lived through meanings, which move towards equilibrium. Your body is not just an object, it is actually all the meanings that people have towards your body."[9] The constant scrutiny, teasing, and taunts aimed in my direction forced out meaning. Using my body, I would chase the approval of boys for much of my adolescence and young adulthood.

A BODY RESTORED

In the Zumba class, I recalled this memory alongside another. I was standing naked in front of the mirror in my bathroom thirty years later, looking at my breasts with a new appreciation. The next day, I would check into my local hospital and my skilled surgeon would cut them from me. They were quite a bit larger and droopier than my prepubescent buds of fifteen. I often made jokes about boob sweat and how I could easily tuck them in the waist of my trousers if I wasn't careful. Wide dark areolas to remind me that I carried two children in my body. Stretch marks like the city streets that circle the Vatican, evidence of the elasticity of skin to hold milk.

Gosh, why did it take me so long to be grateful for "the sisters"? I opened a bottle of anointing oil and made the sign of the cross over each nipple.

"God, who loves bodies so much that you just had to have one, thank you for my breasts. Thank you, dear breasts, for feeding my precious children. Thank you for the many ways you made me feel feminine and powerful and whole."

Back at the rec center, while Julie danced, I walked the track in my body, newly without breasts. Tears began to flow. My pace quickened with the outward-facing anger I now felt toward the boys who would turn me against myself. A holy rage engulfed my body, and I broke into a run, allowing my quads to release the power and pain they had held all these years. My hips held the center as I ran and wailed.

Julie wandered out of Zumba class and found me. I was a striking sight, with mascara smeared all over my tear- and sweat-stained face. My body was tired, and my clothes sopping wet (a byproduct of movement and hot flashes). "Are you okay?" she asked, a look of shock on her face. Honestly, I was never better.

BLESSING BODIES

The reality that God has a body in Jesus comes back to us again during Holy Week and Easter. Jesus, our God who suffers in body and spirit, our God who tasted betrayal of body, wounding of body, dying of body, ultimately experiences resurrection of body. Jesus celebrates his resurrected body through touch. Imagine how healing touch was for Thomas and maybe even Jesus himself (John 20:24-29). Jesus celebrated through tasting a meal; he shared bread and wine with the beloveds on the way to Emmaus and has a fish fry with the disciples on several occasions (Luke 24:13-35, John 21).

What would it look like for you to welcome, honor, and bless your body today? Maybe a long, slow dinner with someone you love, using your senses to savor every moment. Maybe a gentle gaze in the mirror at your body, noticing and giving thanks for all you see. Maybe a simple prayer like, "Jesus, you know about bodies because you've got one. Help me to honor mine as you do."

The following poem is by Daniel Ladinsky. I happened on his little collection titled *I Heard God Laughing*, once while wandering with my children in Powell's bookshop. I read it aloud (as most poems require), we laughed and we cried, which are my two favorite emotions. Dozens of readings later and it still invites me to new levels of bodily healing. Try reading it aloud to someone you love.

CAST ALL YOUR VOTES FOR DANCING

Daniel Ladinsky, drawing on Hafiz

I know the voice of depression
Still calls to you.
I know those habits that can ruin your life
Still send their invitations.
But you are with the Friend now
And look so much stronger.
You can stay that way
And even bloom!
Keep squeezing drops of the Sun
From your prayers and work and music
And from your companions' beautiful laughter.
Keep squeezing drops of the Sun
From the sacred hands and glance of your Beloved
And, my dear,
From the most insignificant movements
Of your own holy body.
Learn to recognize the counterfeit coins
That may buy you just a moment of pleasure,

But then drag you for days
Like a broken man
Behind a farting camel.
You are with the Friend now.
Learn what actions of yours delight Him,
What actions of yours bring freedom
And Love.
Whenever you say God's name, dear pilgrim,
My ears wish my head was missing
So they could finally kiss each other
And applaud all your nourishing wisdom!
O keep squeezing drops of the Sun
From your prayers and work and music
And from your companions' beautiful laughter
And from the most insignificant movements
Of your own holy body.
Now, sweet one,
Be wise.
Cast all your votes for Dancing![10]

Welcoming Practices

Notice. Children have not yet had to split the parts of their person. When they have the feeling of sadness, their bodies cry. When they feel angry, their bodies show it—even if it's at Target during the Christmas rush! They embody an authenticity that we adults often lose. As we grow up, we learn to split the self: we learn to hide our feelings behind our bodies, to ignore the promptings of our spirit. In essence, we teach our parts to speak different messages. Notice when you feel a strong emotion and pause. Notice if your body or spirit is connecting with this emotion.

Re-member your body. Children accept and even celebrate their bodies. Spend some time this week intentionally looking at your body. After a shower in the bathroom mirror, allow your gaze to rest on your body. Notice how time has woven wisdom in your body. What scars or spots tell your life story? If looking at your body is a struggle for you, ask the Spirit to help you see your body through loving eyes. Every body is a sacred body, beloved by God.

Feel your feet. Bodies help us to stay present. Our thoughts and feelings can take us into the past (regret, for example) or the future (anxiety, as another example). Our spirit soars to the external and back again in moments of awe and wonder. But our bodies are just so very present. They are just so *daily*. When we cultivate an awareness of our bodies, they can help us stay present to what is happening before us. A few times a day, draw your attention to your feet. Where your feet are, all of you is invited to be. Wiggle your toes and pray this breath prayer from Psalm 16:1: inhale praying "Protect me, O God," and exhale praying "For in you I take refuge." Notice when your thoughts or feelings are stirred or racing and threaten to take you away from the present. Use this practice to bring you back to the present: allow your feet to literally ground you.

Learn from a book. Read *God Got a Dog* by Cynthia Rylant (illustrated by Marla Frazee). Notice how you feel about the idea that Jesus (God) has a body. Notice the humor and hilarity of that reality. In what ways can you relate to the stories in this book?

5

The Spirituality of Play

Therefore, unmitigated seriousness betokens a lack
of virtue because it wholly despises play, which is
as necessary for a good human life as rest is.

THOMAS AQUINAS

Anwen talked nonstop as we drove to Telluride to ski.[1] She jumped from topic to topic: how skiing felt like flying, why merino wool wasn't itchy, and the loneliness that the pandemic had brought her. I simply listened, savoring the time with my youngest daughter and the mountain landscape that reminded me that beauty still existed. When we arrived, Anwen prepared her gear and I wondered if I put my sunscreen on evenly. (At ten thousand feet above sea level on a sunny day, I will burn like a raw egg on a hot sidewalk.) While my family skied, I sat at an outdoor table reading and writing about play. Yes, the irony was glaring.

In March of 2020, as Covid-19 spread throughout the United States, our lives, like those of many families, took a huge turn. My spouse is an ER physician, so our family locked down immediately.

Anwen, who was fifteen when the pandemic hit, was born into this world full of life and sound. She has been making music since before she could walk. She's people-y, funny, and energetic; for her, the isolation of the pandemic was like the seventh circle of hell. Concerts canceled, friendships suspended—the loss of what gave her life has been extensive. Accompanying her well in this season meant joining her world of movement and sound. In short, it looked like letting her teach us how to play again. Our precious child has had her work cut out for her, though, as the weight of life had crushed much of our playfulness.

Due to an ankle injury, I wasn't able to join them on the slopes, but I did go along to provide snacks and listen to stories. With a gallon of hot tea and a good book, each week I parked myself at an outdoor table watching children and their adults wander by on their way to adventure—each in their own way. Adults, it seems, are anxious to get to the adventure itself; for children, the adventure has no beginning or end. It's all adventure.

The scene was nearly the same each time. Clothed in ski attire, complete with what looked to me like stormtrooper boots, adults led the way while the children wandered behind them. Clearly, the adults were on their way to somewhere, their agenda trying to hurry the pack. Meanwhile, the meandering children loosely followed their parents, stopping and playing in each patch of snow they found. They stomped in it and tasted it. One little one even took his hat off and rubbed the snow in his hair.

On the days that the paths were clear and no snow was to be found, the children experimented with the sound of their boots on the cement walkway. They rocked back and forth from tiptoe to heel; they stomped their feet, listening to the different sounds their boots made on dirt and on the sidewalk. If they noticed my presence, I mimicked their delight or their behavior, raising my eyebrows, smiling, or stomping my own feet. They returned my playful gestures with a giggle or a smile, and we made the gift of human connection. As I watched from the side of the street, I saw that while skiing is a playful sport for adults, children are quicker to slip into the state of play.

A GOD WHO PLAYS

Almost all of us would agree that play is a natural state for children. But I'd suggest we think of play as the natural state of simply living. To play is to be alive. Humans play, animals play, and even God plays. Psalm 104 is an exuberant example of God's playfulness. The psalmist begins with shouts of joy and praise, using imagination to put God's generosity in words.

God is attended by cloud chariots and dancing flames. All of creation, from water to wild animals, is working in harmony with God's good will. The psalm describes an abundance of wine, oil, and bread, all necessary for a fruitful playdate. And then tucked away, almost like a throwaway line, one simple absurd picture is there to shock us—if we are listening—into the playful heart of God. Verse twenty-six contains an unusual verb translated variously as "to sport," "to frolic," or "to romp." Whatever the translation, the verb means something like "to play." Who is doing this play, you may wonder? Only the great monster of the deep, the Leviathan, the most dreaded creature for ancient Hebrews. One translation renders the verse: "Leviathan whom you made to frolic there."[2] Even the Leviathan plays; God who is secure and offers safety to all plays with the Leviathan. Imagine that!

It seems I've always been aware of the playful posture of Jesus, but maybe that's because I met him when I was a child. Reading through the Gospels and getting to know Jesus was an important part of my early formation. Many of the parables that Jesus told were invitations to slip into the state of play. The stories themselves create an imaginary scenario woven with an eternal truth, honoring freedom in the finding of that truth. With play and parable, Jesus helps the listener to suspend their compulsive judging and ever-present ego needs to enter the deeper questions of the soul. We see this in Jesus' explanation of the parable of the sower in Luke 8:11-15. Jesus slips into the state of play and imagination to explore the various outcomes of this parable.

Jesus didn't only *communicate* playfully, he *was* playful. Play is our mother tongue, and Jesus is fluent. We see him enter into play in Matthew 14:22-33. When I read this story, I almost always laugh out loud, which is quite disruptive if I'm reading this lectionary passage before the whole church. The scenes of Jesus putting the disciples into a boat and sending them ahead, of his catching up with them by walking on the lake, of them mistaking him for a ghost, of Peter wanting to join him on the lake, of sinking and the saving: these are all stages of play. Wander with me into the passage.

Like the children who wander behind their parents drinking in all the sights and sounds of their surroundings, Jesus lingered behind the disciples to dismiss the crowd. Afterward, he "went up the mountain by himself to pray" (14:23). I wonder if this time savoring his place at the heart of his Father gave him the ability to enter into playful engagement with his friends on the lake. Did his experience of being a child resting in the safety and security of his Father provide the freedom to play a bit?

Imagine with me the courage it took for Jesus to step out on the lake in the middle of a storm. We are told that the boat was battered by the waves and the wind was against them. What a glorious absurdity it is to step into a storm from the safety of the shore. Play often employs a level of absurdity. We are free to tinker with absurdity when our safety is grounded in God. This was the case for Jesus. He could imagine the unimaginable because he knew himself to be safe in his Father's care.

Next, he walked on the water, toward his friends. His very presence was engaging and invited his friends' emotional expression: they cried out that they'd seen a ghost. All of us carry around childhood fears of what we don't understand and can't control. These fears are easily thumped and pulled into the present when we are adults. From his own sense of being a child in the bosom of the Father, Jesus responds to their fear with his presence, saying, "It is I; do not be afraid" (14:27). It is I, the I AM, who longed each one into being and who will never abandon. The I AM who was with Eve and Adam, whose very name, Emmanuel, means "God with us." These scared and seasick beloveds were the children of I AM. Therefore, they had no need to fear, even though they did.

It's at this point in the story where I wish we had some understanding of what was physically happening. How were the disciples holding their bodies at this moment? What did they do with their hands, their feet? What were their facial expressions? What was the look on Jesus' face?

It seems to me that Jesus slipped into a state of play and Peter responded. I have often heard it preached that Peter came to Jesus out of fear, but I don't think so. We human beings simply don't leave a place of safety (the boat) for a place of danger (walking on the whirling, windy water). Did Jesus wink, did the edges of his mouth curl up, did he wave Peter out onto the lake? What bodily signal did Jesus send to Peter that said, "While we're out here, we might as well have a bit of fun. Wanna give this a try?"

Peter cautiously accepted Jesus' offer to play and stepped out of the boat. Notice that the storm had not ceased. It was just as dangerous and just as absurd as it was when Jesus stepped out onto it. Jesus' presence offered Peter the safety he needed, and he went for it. I wonder how long the two of them were playing on the water together before Peter's fears stirred and gobbled up his attention and connection? Peter began to sink, and Jesus immediately caught him and restored his sense of safety.

Jesus' next words are pure playful genius. In keeping with the loving, generous, welcoming presence of God, Jesus brought levity to the event by calling Peter a pet name, "Little Faith," and then asking a question dripping with absurdity: "Why did you doubt?" These words can seem judgmental and even condemning, but only if we take them outside of the playful loving tone of God, our Divine Parent.

Could it be that Jesus was using a bit of ironic humor here? I mean, why wouldn't a person doubt? They were walking on water, and there's a principle about the three states of matter . . . and there's a storm raging . . . and, well, people can't breathe under water. What if Jesus was playing and inviting Peter to play too? Maybe, through humor, Jesus was putting Peter at ease by reminding him of the absurdity of the moment and the gift of his playful presence within it.

I think Jesus and Peter played together on the water, playing in a way that flowed from love and not fear. When Peter was afraid, he fell out of play. But Jesus didn't leave him to sink in his fear and in the water. Jesus reassured him and then invited him back into play. Their encounter was simply an opportunity to connect, to be together. There seems to be no agenda in this encounter. Peter didn't go on to be a famous water walker.

WHAT IS PLAY?

Play is a creative state of being where the inner and outer life can mingle without the pressure to perform, plan, or achieve. For children, it is natural; for adults, it must be intentional. Our spiritual and emotional health depends on our ability to play throughout all the developmental stages of life. Playing relieves our stress and improves brain function. And playing with others is deeply connective. We learn to cooperate, read social cues, and enjoy the company of another. Play opens new creative possibilities: it offers us the freedom to fail.

Play is an active state of being. We flow in and out of this state based on our needs and the safety we perceive around us. We (children and adults) can only move into the state of play when we feel safe and secure. Play's grace is process and potential: during play we can process our wounds and wonder about potential futures. Clinical psychologist Dr. Gordon Neufeld, who studies attachment and the importance of true play, suggests that true play has several particular characteristics.[3]

According to Dr. Neufeld's work, play is engaging and expressive. We can easily think of play and fun as being exclusively intertwined, but that's not so. Play can produce warm and happy feelings, but those feelings are not necessary to play itself. Rather, play is a state that allows us to engage with the outside world *and* our inner life. Play is the state where these two realities come together. For a child, play can look like working out anxiety around the first day of school by running Hot Wheels cars into each other. Play can look like singing an impromptu song about loving the family dog. These are both acts of creation, bringing inside realities to bear on the outside world. Mr. Rogers famously taught children how to express their inside feelings in an outside way by using sounds on the piano.[4]

Play for adults can look like taking a Zumba class and working out our work frustrations with a shake of our hips. Play can look like a game of hoops with the president of the United States.[5]

Play is not outcome based. Play is not for keeps. Play is its own reward simply because it helps us to escape the pressure of outcomes and the constant clamoring of self-awareness. While growing self-awareness is a good thing, it can also become a compulsion that rarely offers us a break from ourselves. True play is a state of being in which it is safe to lay down our ever-pressing need to mind ourselves. It is a state where our beingness is free to emerge with emotion and or wonder. Play is a state where we can try on potential outcomes, test out ideas, practice scenarios, and not be governed by permanence. When children play, they exercise the capacity to imagine different possibilities in their world. Play offers a break from reality giving us freedom from old patterns. Creativity soars during play. As play therapist Di Gammage writes, "Play is the innate gift we are born with, through which we not only make discoveries but can also challenge our findings. Play allows us to dissolve what we think we know to make space for something new and thus far unknown."[6]

One last interesting aspect of play is that it has a beginning and an ending. Play has boundaries, which is why it is safe enough to be free. Play is not a static state but fluid and dynamic. We slip into and out of it with ease when we are healthy. When we play with others, we send signals that we are playing. Those signals, when clearly sent and received, communicate safety, humility, and an invitation to connection. When the signal is accepted and play erupts, the connection between both parties deepens.

In my childhood home, it was the kids' job to wash the dishes after dinner. My mother cooked, and we all ate, but my brother and I cleaned up. I can't remember the circumstances around the dinner conversation, but I do remember that it was a hard social season at school for me. My brother, four years my junior, typically disappeared into the bathroom just as the cleaning started, which increased my disgruntled teenager vibe. Feeling frustrated at home and frustrated at school left me moody and just not a lot of fun to be around. After dinner, my father and brother both left the table, and I sat with my mom, a heavy heart, and a few uneaten potatoes. I remember looking at my plate, trying to decide whether I should begin to clear the table or whether I should bang on the bathroom door protesting my plight.

Amid my angst, I saw movement in my mother's direction and looked up just in time to see a grape coming right at my forehead. A huge smile spread across my mom's face as she loaded her spoon with the sparse leftover potatoes and shot them in my direction. I returned her smile, held up my napkin as a shield, and began to load my own spoon with the remnants of my brother's plate—carefully excluded onions in a tidy pile. There wasn't much food left after dinner, but the bits that were littered the tiny kitchen. I still laugh as I think of that memory. It was a moment of connection through play between my mother and myself. She made a space for me to express my emotions—by flinging onion bits in her general direction. Her playfulness and humility gave me a break from myself and the compulsive tending of my troubled thoughts. It reminded me of our connection and the grace of not being alone.

PLAYING WITH GOD

So, what does it look like to play with God? My dear friend Dave is play incarnate. Here's a story he tells about fishing with God in

Oregon. Notice the movements of play and connection. What invitations within you are stirred?

Today I'm going fishing with my Dad [God]. The sun is shining, and Mt. Hood is beautiful in the distance. It is a bit misty, colder than I had hoped, but here we are and, so, off we go. I launch the boat, throw in my gear, and begin the day. I row back and forth just off the boat ramp, thinking maybe the fish are holed up here. No luck. My favorite spot has always been across the lake between the bench and the fallen tree. So, I put on my bigger lure and troll across the lake.

As soon as I get to the "spot," I am slammed by a big one. It surprised me because I wasn't really expecting anything of size. Most of the fish I catch here are in the ten to twelve inch range. This one almost pulled my pole out of the boat. I reeled him close to the boat, tried to maneuver the net and pole, got him right up to the side . . . and lost him. Dang! It was as big a trout as I've ever caught at this lake and of course I was immediately disappointed.

But then I heard my Father (I heard because I was listening), "Hey, it's early. Let's stay right here and fish a while. Perhaps you'll catch another big one." Good advice, I thought. It was then that I noted that I wasn't fishing alone. I was fishing with my Dad.

I threw back in and started trolling again. Down to the bench and then back to the spot. Bang! Fish on. This time I was ready and pulled him into the boat. It was a big one, twenty inches or more for sure. The limit is five fish per day, and only one over twenty inches. This was easily that or more. Then, I measured it. Nope. Eighteen and a half. Fisherman's eyes, they always make things appear larger! Maybe a pound and a half. A keeper for sure. Good one, God! . . . Good one.

Trolling down and back, and once again at the spot—Pow! Another one on the line. This one feels bigger than the last. He's jumping out of the water, spinning around as I am reeling him towards the boat. What a hoot! I'm not sure my net is big enough for this one. Twenty inches? No, seventeen. Close to two pounds though. I seldom catch one this size and now I've caught two!?

I stop for a second. I look toward my Father. He has on that big smile. Thank you, God, this is such fun. "I know, it's fun for me too. Now quit talking and keep fishing!" he responds playfully. I caught five more in the next hour, kept two and released the others. The biggest was over eighteen inches, chubby, again easily over two pounds.

I stopped for lunch. What a beautiful day. The sun was out and the wind had died down. I sat in the boat, reflecting on my morning with Dad and we talked about how grateful I am for days like this, His friendship, and how much fun it is. He agreed. Four fish in three hours, all about eighteen inches, and sunshine and beautiful scenery to boot!

We fished a while more and didn't catch anything. Time to go. That's enough for one day. I'll troll back across the lake. If I catch another, fine. If not, what a day! When I got to the boat launch, some kayakers were just putting in so I had to pause and give them some space. I'll just troll back and forth while I wait.

Pow. Surprise! I've got another fish on! And a big one at that. As I got the fish right to the boat he pulled away, one last attempt to free himself from the hook. Sure enough, he broke loose. Oh no! I panicked and swiped my net through the water in a weird "hopeless" attempt at maybe snagging him before he swam away in victory. He fell right into the net, right into the boat. The twenty-incher of the day!

I paused and couldn't help but laugh. A perfect ending to a perfect day.

"Thanks Dad. I had a great time," I said to God. "Me too, Son. Let's do it again soon!" he responded.[7]

Notice a few things about Dave's fishing trip. First, he is fully present to his surroundings through his body, which helps him to be aware of God's invitations for connection. Dave also sets his intention to listen for God and expects that he will indeed encounter God, which he does. Dave doesn't shirk from the playful invitations that he hears from God; instead, he surrenders his own agenda and even the management of his own perceptions. He slips into child's play and his attachment to God deepens.

BENEFITS OF PLAY

Playfulness is an avenue to our well-being. Play helps adults to break free from our compulsions to judge and analyze. Play reconnects us with the foundational generosity of Genesis, which is the truest form of our existence as God's beloved children. Our various human drives do not affect us equally.[8] When our survival needs are not met or we perceive that we are in danger, play will disappear. We cannot play and live in fear at the same time.

Children learn who they are through play. Adults tend to live as though who we are has hardened, but that's not inevitable. The Spirit, our Holy Knitter, continues to knit us, perhaps into eternity, gathering up all the bits of goodness and glory. And play can change our lives, even as adults. Play reminds us that life is fluid and dynamic. Play offers us the gift of potentiality. It happens between the spaces of who we think we are and who we think we are not. Play greases the wheels of our longings and gives us a chance to live them out. Play serves our life with God in that it breaks the old, corroded patterns of the life we want to walk beyond and gives us a vision of the life we want to have. Play's social aspect fosters empathy. Play is the core of all right-brain acts like creativity and innovation. Play helps us to problem-solve without pressure to perform.[9] Play helps us to adapt to the world around us by harnessing the power of pleasure.

Admittedly, play packs a larger neurological reward for children than it does for adults. The adult brain is not developing as rapidly and so our drive for varied experiences is less. But that doesn't mean that we don't need play. Without it we more easily fall into depression and a general sense of hopelessness. Theorist Brian Sutton-Smith quoted in Brown's *Play* reminds us that the opposite of play is not work, but depression.[10] Moreover, as we age, play creates much-needed neural connections. It keeps our brains and bodies healthy and flexible. For adults, activities like music, dancing, and painting can serve the beneficial role of play; they involve the brain and the body, inviting us to connect with community through vulnerability and a playful posture.

During the pandemic, Anwen taught me how to play. It looks like taking myself more lightly and connecting more deeply. She has taught me how to laugh and how to set my work aside and enjoy a game of "cat pong": Ping-Pong at the kitchen table, but with the help of our two cats, Mama Kitty and Useless. (Yes, of course, she named them.)

The spiritual practice of play frees us for transformation. It bypasses our hardened categories and habits and opens us to new possibilities. Play can help us to work out our fears, to bring them to our Divine Parent and receive a healing presence. True play is also energizing; it can bring life and levity to situations we have become numb to. Play produces a reciprocal energy that comes from the willingness of those who are playing. It can help us to awake to joy and wonder before us. A saying attributed to Jesuit mystic Pierre Teilhard de Chardin describes joy this way: "Joy is the infallible sign of the presence of God."[11]

By the age of seven most children will be fully skilled in all methods of play. But if you are over seven, don't worry—these skills are still within you.

Poetry can be play. Moving words and phrases around, shaping nuance, pulling from the past, present, and future to work out, sometimes with fear and trembling, the truth: this can be playful. In the early months of 2021, I lived in the poem "Go to the Limits of Your Longing," written by Rainer Maria Rilke.[12] I prayed it with my directees, shared it with my friends, and was surprised by it when watching a children's movie. One night, when Anwen and I were feeling weighed down by the many pandemic losses, we watched Disney's *Flora and Ulysses* together. As we don't have a TV in our home (a smart trade I made with my spouse when he wanted a motorcycle and I wanted to get rid of the TV), we watch movies on our computers. Anwen found the movie and we snuggled up in her bed with popcorn, a laptop, and each other's company. About ten minutes in, I realized that there was something familiar about the movie.

"Have we seen this?" I asked.

"Oh, jeez, Mom," Anwen said. "We read the book when I was about ten years old."

"Did we like it?" I wondered, as for me, the overexaggerated antics in children's movies tend to bring on involuntary eye rolling followed by nausea.

We continued with the movie and I remembered some parts, but there was another level of familiarity I couldn't put my finger on. When the neighbor character, Tootie, read Rilke's poem to Ulysses, a squirrel with superhero powers and a penchant for poetry, the pieces came together. The poem "Go to the Limits of Your Longing" was to mark the advent of his transformation. Maybe the poem was resonating with my own transformation, or perhaps my longing for it.

Even as I lived in the poem over many weeks, there was one word I wanted to play with. One word that seems to push against what I continue to learn about God, about the world, and about myself. In the next-to-last line of the poem, Rilke writes that we will know life "by its seriousness."[13] Respectfully, and speaking as someone still in the process of transformation, I disagree, dear Rilke. We will know true life by its playfulness.

Welcoming Practices

Reflect on delight. Go back to your childhood altar. Look with love and compassion on your childhood self. What is something that you delighted in doing when you were a child? What is something that you did simply because it was fun? Think back through different stages of your life, beginning as far back as you can, and tell your stories of the ways that you enjoyed playing. Maybe it's time to relaunch an old hobby?

Play with God. Get outside. Take a nature walk and notice how the earth plays. Kick around the leaves, stomp your feet in a puddle, draw your attention to the wind. Notice the animals, wild and otherwise. What can you learn from them about play? Choose a specific amount of time (twenty to thirty minutes) to move with God. Notice what of yourself you feel free to offer and notice what feels reserved. You can also play with God in art. *Come Look with Me: World of Play* by Gladys S. Blizzard is a guided look at various art depicting play. Invite the Spirit to come and look with you at how artists throughout history see play.

Learn from a book. Read *Flora and Ulysses: The Illuminated Adventures* by Kate DiCamillo aloud. Notice who you most resonate with in the story.

6

Fountain Flowing Deep and Wide

*Deep within us all there is an amazing inner sanctuary
of the soul, a holy place, a Divine Center, a speaking Voice,
to which we may continuously return. Eternity is at our hearts,
pressing upon our time-torn lives, warming us with intimations
of an astounding destiny, calling us home unto Itself.*

THOMAS R. KELLY

"Deep and Wide" is a familiar children's song sung at children's camps and children's churches far and wide. To sing it one must use both body and soul, which is exactly how children sing. When singing the word *deep*, children lift one arm up as high as they can, while simultaneously dropping the other arm as low as they can. When singing the word *wide*, children open up their arms as far as the east is from the west—often whacking their neighbor in playful delight. It's got a catchy tune and the lyrics couldn't be truer: "Deep and wide, deep and wide. There's a fountain flowing deep and wide" (×2).

This song was written by Sidney Cox, who was a major in the Salvation Army.[1] Cox wrote verses, but I've never heard them sung. Apparently, they reference Ezekiel 47:1-12, where streams of living water flow from God's temple, bringing life to all that surrounds. The passage begins with Ezekiel's angelic guide, "the man," wading in the water ever deeper. First, the water is to his ankles, then to his knees, then his waist, and then, so deep he could only swim. When he leads Ezekiel along the riverbank, Ezekiel sees that this living water feeds "a great many trees" that sustain and heal the people. Every living creature benefits from this stream. The stream of God's love is deep and wide, much deeper than we can see or understand (Ephesians 3:18-19). Can you ever find the bottom of God's love? Nope. Can you ever push the edges of God's love? Nope.

Over the years as I have sung this song and pondered its meaning; it just gets better and better. It gets, well . . . wider and deeper. I'm not saying that all my years of formal study have been a waste, but most of what's important is right here, in this simple children's song. Hear me out.

When we are children, our awareness of God, others, and self, is wide. We have a million first encounters. Everything is new and wonder-filled, including our encounters with God. We can describe these experiences with the helpful word *cataphatic*. Cataphatic is a theological term referring to definitions of God that are based on what God is, rather than what God is not. So, cataphatic experiences ignite our senses and sanctify our imaginations. We see, touch, taste, smell, and hear. We are filled with words, images, symbols, and ideas. Cataphatic experiences of God are expansive, and children are the experts. The human brain is drawn to new experiences, and since most experiences are new to children, their style of engagement with the world, most of the time, is wide rather than deep.[2]

A WIDE JOY

God, as the wooer of every human soul, draws us with every good. Joy is the main fruit of wide experience. And of course it is—God is joyful. Do we think that God experiences pleasure? What have we been taught about pleasure?

Christian philosopher Dallas Willard writes,

> We should, to begin with, think that God leads a very interesting life, and that he is full of joy. Undoubtedly, he is the most joyous being in the universe. The abundance of his love and generosity is inseparable from his infinite joy. All of the good and beautiful things from which we occasionally drink tiny droplets of soul-exhilarating joy, God continuously experience in all their breadth and depth and richness.[3]

C. S. Lewis called joy "the serious business of heaven," and we can catch a glimpse of it in Luke 10:21-24.[4] Jesus and his friends have been working. They've been doing the faithful work of preaching, healing, and generally loving on others. (Yes, yes, I know that earlier in this chapter, Jesus teaches his friends about healthy boundaries. He also has some very strong words for cities that continue to sleep even as they are invited to wake up. These are still acts of love.) In verses 17-20, the friends are coming home from a work trip, and they are joyous. The trip went well, and they can't wait to tell about their adventures with God. Jesus reciprocates their joy. Joy begets joy. Joy tastes best when shared with others.

Verse 21 tells us that "Jesus rejoiced in the Holy Spirit." Just let that sink in a minute. Jesus rejoices. Jesus is shot through with joy and delight. Jesus, who has tasted both the fullness of heaven and the dusty streets of Jerusalem, rejoices. And he rejoices in the Holy Spirit: he shares joy with his most intimate community, love's family, the trinitarian community of love.

One of the most joyous occasions in Western society is a child's first birthday. It is a celebration of the little one in particular, but also a celebration of all that the parents and family have been through in the previous year. It is no small task to arrive at year one. Like the disciples, we parents may have battled our own demons just to make it this far. During the celebration we take thousands of photographs of children with cake smashed into their hair, nose, and ears. The delight and pure joy of the first year touches a place inside all of us that longs to be free of habitual patterns of living. We long to have the capacity to maintain delight in our earthy existence. We are hungry to take it all in again.

In this passage Jesus spoke to his community of love, offering thanks that the Father has revealed "hidden" things to infants that remain hidden to the rest of us. What is it that children know that adults do not? Likely there are many things, but maybe one is delight in earthly—or earthy—things. Young children have not grown bored with the ordinary, but delight in the smallest things: ladybugs, dryer lint, and rocks. Just take a toddler on a walk and you'll find yourself fishing all sorts of things out of their hands and mouths. They are eager to experience all that surrounds them with every dimension of their person.

When my children were young, we ambled down our graveled driveway to check the mail. Over and over, for what seemed like hours to my older and weary soul, we followed their delight. They examined each rock, seeing each as an incalculable treasure. They were eager to show me every wandering line, every unremarkable sparkle, and every conjured imagination. When they named where they "saw God" just before bedtime, it was always in the ordinary and earthy. Big Ma's peach jam, the cold wet nose of our dog Lilly, snowflakes, and bubbles in the bathtub. Notice the delight children have for the earthy. How can you let their delight open you to the rejoicing of Jesus, of Love's family? What hidden-in-plain-sight glories are you missing?

A DEEP FAITH

Yes, as children, we have a wide experience of God; but there is also a deep. As we age, our conscious engagement narrows and deepens. We can see this process beginning even in childhood, when children become absorbed in a topic. (There are many stories of God encounters from children that have to do with the finer points of horses, trains, dinosaurs, and, more recently, Pokémon and Minecraft.) This curiosity makes a way for deepening. Our absorbed curiosities take up brain space. So in order to store that curiosity, we need to shift some of our experiences away from our conscious mind and toward unconscious habit.

The habits we develop thankfully free us up to focus more deeply, but in gaining these habits, we lose the wide and wonderful consciousness of simple encounters. For example, when toothbrushing (a sensory experience for sure) becomes habit, it frees up space and time to become absorbed in a topic of our curiosity, like grasshoppers. To quote Winnie the Pooh, we are "Bears of Very Little Brain." Initially, we simply can't hold both the wide and the deep. The movements between wide and deep and back again stretch and strengthen our experience of our infinite God.

Sometimes our experiences of God move to the *apophatic*—
the opposite of cataphatic. We experience God in the negative.
We learn what God is not. We taste hatred and harm and learn
that God is not that. In moments of radical love and tender pain,
we experience God in what is not there, solitude and in silence.
Where there is no sight, sound, touch, taste, or smell of God's
presence, we find that God is there too, but in ways that are totally
new to us. Our hunger for the cataphatic (sensory) when there is
little evidence in our lives for God, drives us deeper into the apophatic experience (silence and solitude) where words and images
are few.

In the third half of life (math is hard), when we welcome our
childlike selves, the invitation is to maintain the depth and regain
the expansiveness of the everyday. As adults we can choose the
binary, either deep or wide. But it seems our playful God is inviting
us to follow Jesus into the deep *and* wide. We are born to the cataphatic, we learn the apophatic, and now the invitation is to play
with freedom within them both.

Maybe this is what Jesus' conversation with Nicodemus was
about (John 3). Nicodemus at one time was a child and had a full
experience of wide faith. He grew up and followed to deep faith;
he was a Pharisee, a religious leader, one who studied, tested, and
tried. But there was just something about Jesus. Jesus is wholeness,
the wide and the deep as One. Nicodemus also knew that in a
world of either/or, in/out, wrong/right, meeting with Jesus was
dangerous. So he came at night to ask the questions that burned
in his soul. "How can anyone be born after having grown old?"
and "Can one enter a second time into the mother's womb and
be born?" (John 3:4). The second birth is the one that combines
the wideness of our childhood with the depth of our adulthood.

Maybe being "born again" is welcoming both the Christ child and the child within us.

One of the early games that children play with adults is peekaboo. It is especially delightful for the child, who is filled with giggles as the adult hides and then reappears. Child psychologists tell us that this form of play is essential for children, whose greatest fear is abandonment. The repetitive play of "Where is Mama?" and then "There she is!" confronts the child's fear indirectly through play and reinforces confidence that the parent will return. Absence is not permanent. Absence is perception, not lasting reality. Perhaps play in the spiritual life looks like this too. Through play, the Spirit accompanies us as we indirectly face our fears. We learn that God is never absent from us.

Could it be similar to our experience of what Saint John of the Cross and others call the dark night? In this "dark night," God's presence seems to go missing, and our connection with God and reality shifts. We struggle to hear, see, or feel God. We wonder, *Where has God gone?* Our sensory experience tells us that God is not present, but, as the psalmist reminds us, there is no place that God is not (Psalm 139). When the dark night recedes, we notice that our trust in God has deepened, our picture of God has shifted, and we will never be the same. The great monster of abandonment has been tamed, and now we know that while our senses do dial us into God's presence, they aren't the anchor of reality. The reality of God's love, we learn, holds us even in silence and absence.

ABSORBED IN THE DEEP AND WIDE

Play has the distinct advantage of lowering our defenses. The survival skills that developed from our woundedness have a shelf life.

Their help only lasts as long as it doesn't begin to box us in and lock us up. Play can bypass our compulsive attachment to our defenses and open us to new ways of engaging with others and the world. Play can usher us into the realm where our inner and outer life are one. Irish poet John O'Donohue reminds us that "each person is always on the threshold between their inner world and their outer world, between light and darkness, between known and unknown, between question and quest, between fact and possibility."[5] Play's superpower is that it dissolves the threshold and the two worlds become one. Play helps us to be present in both worlds at once.

Children's playful posture situates them to enjoy at times a deep union with God. Their way of being is both before and beyond consciousness. Play requires freedom from the preoccupation of self-management, which produces a sincerity that makes way for moments of union. Explorations of playful creativity can shift us adults into this way.

For several years, our family was part of an ecumenical, multiethnic, intergenerational small group. Our rhythm was engaging with good food, good conversation, and our good God. During times of reflection, we would drag out a huge plastic box of LEGO bricks. The children were invited to use them to craft their response to the reflection question. Sometimes they did just that. Other times, they followed their curiosity and created something else altogether brilliant. Both options were welcome, and we made space to listen to their descriptions of their creations and their process. What I most noticed was that when the children were really tuned in, they were totally absorbed in their playful creating. They easily entered into a creative space with God, free to ignore the adults and play with what was before them.

We adults often withhold our full engagement in the moment due to our ever-present managing. It restricts our capacity to enter play fully, with all the dimensions of our selves. No one plays *partly*. In the same way, Christian mysticism requires full engagement, a radical giving of self to God who loves our souls into existence. Children, with their natural playfulness, easily give their whole selves to whatever is before them. Their ability to play is due in part to the freedom they experience at not having to manage their inner baggage.

Years ago, a dear friend asked me about the spiritual practice of play in my own life. You'd think the answer would be easy. I have been a teacher of children since I was twelve, which is when I taught my first Girls in Action class. I was a babysitting machine in high school and college. I went to college to study English and be an elementary educator. I have taught children in Texas, New York, Kazakhstan, Colorado, and many places in between. Further, when I'm out and about, I'm drawn to children. I like them. I like the things they say. I like the way they communicate through their bodies. I like the way they see the world. When my friend asked me the question, I had been engaging with children most of my life; surely I had engaged in their signature way of being in the world.

But I answered honestly: I couldn't remember the last time I played. Certainly, I have been gifted with a playful nature, but I rarely experience the freedom of absorption and self-forgetfulness. I have attended play groups, planned playdates, cleaned up after playing, and even pretended to play. Then my friend asked me a simple question that was to unhinge the next season of my life. He asked, "What did you do for fun when you were a child?"

Well, I spent the entire fourth grade writing sermons on three-by-five index cards instead of doing my schoolwork. Fun? During preschool and kindergarten, I learned to work the cash register and wait on customers in my grandparents' deli. Fun? Maybe I needed a more precise question. "When, as a child, did you delight in something so much that you lost track of time?" That's an easy answer: I rarely lose track of time. I'm über-punctual and feel guilty when I'm not.

The word *delight* is a curious word, meaning "great happiness or pleasure." While I was speaking with my friend, I realized that I struggled to wrap my mind around delight. What did delight me? I began to pray, asking God to bring to my mind a memory of great delight and play. God answered generously; a flood of memories came back.

One in particular has been shedding light and helping to guide me in my current season of life. I remember sitting on my dad's lap, picking the dirt from between my toes and listening to the adults tell stories from their lives. We were at an outside gathering with lots of adults and some children. Some stories were funny, some were sad, and, if I know this bunch, maybe some of them were even true. I had on a green plaid bikini (be kind, it was the 1970s) and was wrapped in a towel after playing in the lake all day. I heard stories about bathroom pranks in outhouses and about late-night taunts in the woods.

It was the first time I learned about my dad serving in the Vietnam War, along with several of his cousins. It was also the first time I learned that my grandmother had a metal rod in her arm from a terrible car accident. This memory has helped me realize that for me, play often looks like listening to people tell their stories, and sometimes even telling a few of my own. I lose all track of time and sense of self. I am absorbed in what is between us, the sharing of life, the wide and the deep. How about you? What did you do when you were young that filled you with delight?

FALLACY OF THE SLIPPERY SLOPE

Play in the spiritual life might feel a little risky. We might wonder if we are taking the God of the universe seriously enough, or if we should be doing things that seem more ascetic. Thomas Kelly writes, "The Cross as dogma is painless speculation; the Cross as lived suffering is anguish and glory."[6] Play moves the faith of our head out to our bodies. We can house our faith in our heads with very little risk, but we will also have very little life. Play invites us to jump all in with our whole bodies and souls. It invites us to risk what we don't know or can't see for abundant life with the God who truly loves us.

We might fear that if we play, if we go all in, we will slip down the slope and all our fears will become realized. But as someone has said (and goodness me, I wish I could remember who it was!), the slippery slope is only a danger if we are swimming in the shallow end. In the shallow end, if we slip, we can easily crack our heads. But in the deep and wide sea of God's love, a slip is only a slide. It's purely child's play.

Welcoming Practices

Sing songs. Go back to the songs of your childhood. Perhaps begin with "Deep and Wide." Sing and sit with these songs for a bit. Listen for the wisdom that might be there for you in this season of your life. If you didn't grow up with childhood songs of truth and light, it's not too late to learn some. Try Twila Paris's album *Bedtime Prayers: Lullabies and Peaceful Worship* or any of the three albums from Rain for Roots.

Experiment in cataphatic and apophatic prayer. Begin with cataphatic prayer by making your favorite meal with people you love. Choose the best ingredients you can afford and ask those you love to help you cut, chop, cook, and create. During this time, let your shared conversation be around what you see, touch, taste, smell, and hear. Open a group conversation with God about your experience. Speak as though God is present—because God is. Apophatic prayer is less responsive to our actions; it's more like unmerited grace that shows up when you were looking elsewhere. And it takes time, lots of time. Choose a time of the day just before dawn or after dusk when you can be alone. Sit in an upright position and allow yourself to become aware of God's presence. You may not feel God's presence in the ways you have felt God in the past. That's okay. You can just say, "I know you're here." When thoughts come into your mind, let them go and come back to "I know you're here." Stay with this kind of prayer, letting God meet you in the silence and solitude. For more guidance on the apophatic practice of centering prayer read Frank X. Jelenek and Ann Boyajian's book *Journey to the Heart: Centering Prayer for Children.*

Learn from a book. Read *Seeking Aurora*, written by Elizabeth Pulford and illustrated by Anne Bannock. Is there an adventure, an aurora that the Father is inviting you to? Or enter into Max Lucado and T. Lively Fluharty's beautiful book *The Boy and the Ocean.* Is there a cataphatic or apophatic invitation emerging for you?

7

Imaginate

Reason is the natural organ of truth;
but imagination is the organ of meaning.

C. S. LEWIS

I have known Matthew for nearly his whole life, and he continues to teach me. We met through his mother, Jeannette. In my early twenties, she spent two years patiently walking with me through Richard Foster's *Celebration of Discipline*. The Spirit, the holy weaver, used this book and Jeannette's faithful presence to reweave for me a deeper and more authentically true relationship with God. Little Matthew, her youngest son, was only in elementary school at the time, so he'd come with her to our weekly meetings and play outside. Matthew loves to be outside. His imagination has free rein in nature, and even now, at twenty-eight years old, he uses it to its full potential. Once, when he overheard me talking with his mother about a struggle in my life, he shared a bit of wisdom. "Lacy," he said, with all the humility of his eight years, "you should imaginate." He offered me his stuffed animals and invited me to imagine possibilities beyond my rational knowing. From the lips of babes, right?

Young children use their imaginative powers for good. Often when I lead adults through an experience of using their imaginations, I hear a bit of pushback around their perceived "lack of imagination." One simple question generally helps us get in touch with reality: "Do you ever worry?"

Worry and its cousin, anxiety, are products of imagination at the service of fear. But young children use their imagination in the service of wonder, curiosity, exploration, and play. They can tap into the creative goodness woven within each person to work through problems and find solutions for the future. For children, imagination is common and glorious. It is play and creativity on steroids. It is one way children embody the image of our God, who is effortlessly and endlessly imaginative.

JESUS AND IMAGINATION

It's easy to see imagination at work in Jesus. For one example, let's take a look at John 6. It is just before Passover and Jesus has been teaching, healing, and generally being with large crowds of people. He is tired from the day's good work but is not blind to the ongoing needs of the people: it's late and they need to eat. Jesus asks an absurd question, one that is typical of those who embody the holy foolishness of God. "Where are we to buy bread for these people to eat?" (John 6:5).

Can you imagine that? The Bread of Life purchasing bread? If John was right and this was a test, the fellas got a D- in imagination. Philip whips out his calculator (not actually . . . work with me here) and realizes that there's just not enough money. Andrew's first instinct is his best: "There is a boy here who has five barley loaves and two fish," he begins. But his simple faith and childlike imagination are overwhelmed by scarcity as he concludes, "But what are they among so many people?" (John 6:9).

It's here that my own imagination sparks. What happens within Jesus at this moment? Does the creative joy of his life in the Trinity make his pulse race? How many possibilities begin to unfold in his mind? Does a playful smirk come across his face as he lets his mind wander through all the delight and fun that's about to open up? I wonder if he feels a little like I feel each Christmas Eve when I fill the kids' stockings with chocolates and other goodies. I just can't wait to see their faces. I laugh aloud and even talk to myself imagining the fun we'll have. Did Jesus have an inner conversation with the Father and the Spirit? Did they, in a split second, sort out all the options—which would be the most joyous, the most fun, and the most filled with surprise? When Jesus said, "Make the people sit down," did he offer a spirited wink toward the boy?

After the people sit down, he feeds them, *all* of them, with this kid's lunch. They eat until they are filled, and, if that's not enough, the leftovers are gathered into twelve baskets, enough to almost exhaust my grandmother's Cool Whip container collection. There had to be laughing and sharing and talking. Here the Bread of Life multiplies bread where there is little. Generosity beats out scarcity and wonder wins the day. Joy flows from the trinitarian community of love and everyone eats.

IMAGINING PERIL AND POSSIBILITY

Imagination is the DNA of symbolism and sacred rituals that can help us work through our fears and open us to the possibilities that God might be inviting us into. Sending my kids off to college after homeschooling them for nearly two decades surfaced a mixture of celebration and fear for me. When we left Aidan at college to study environmental engineering, I felt like I was leaving part of my heart there too. I sobbed the entire six-hour drive home. As Aidan found freedom, so did I. I missed my beloved oldest child, but it's been a good missing.

One evening, just before Aidan was to come home for a visit, I got a phone call. "Uh, Mom," Aidan stammered, "I just want you to know that I got a tattoo." Now, tattoos are not new to our family. My brother has a collection of strikingly beautiful tats he got when he was a Marine serving in Okinawa. He also has two stars, a red and a green one on either side of his collarbones, memorials to two children he pulled from a house fire when he was a firefighter. I know that tattoos can be sacred art, a collective cocreation, marking events and periods of our living. Before Aidan went to college, we had a long discussion around Aidan's growing desire for a tattoo of the dragon Toothless from the animated movie *How to Train Your Dragon*. Aidan was feeling the coming shift in relationship with Anwen, and Toothless was a reminder of their shared relationship and love. I surely understood the logic and had some empathy for Aidan's desire, but felt triumphant when the subject was no longer in play.

"You did?" I said, working to weave wonder into my response. "What did you get?"

"Captain America's broken shield," Aidan said, "on my right shoulder blade."

Listening helped me understand the image's meaning both in the Marvel story and in Aidan's lived experience. The shield represented Aidan's first real understanding of the state of our beloved planet. As an environmental engineer in training, constantly learning how devastating the facts and figures are, especially for the least of these in our world, can be overwhelming. Battling to stay engaged in a field that finds few successes and mostly uncovers bad news is hard on the soul. The tattoo was a cocreative piece of art, a marked reminder to stay with it even if there is no triumphant outcome. It's a reminder of Aidan's faithfulness. Imagination is an ordinary superpower, and I pray that it will help Aidan find creative possibilities and dream for a restorative future.

Imagination can help us to notice and name the peril we see coming. It can also help us to listen to the wisdom whispered by the Spirit who longs to bring about healing to all creation. Imagination helps us to groan together with the Spirit for those who suffer in our world. The Spirit seems to be right at home working with our imaginations, coupling lived experience with courageous responses.

IMAGINATION'S TIGHTROPE WALK

"But we're not children; we're adults. Imagination is childish."

It was a small slip of a conversation that I mistakenly overheard as I left the women's restroom. (Seriously, who rests in there?) I had just finished giving my annual teaching to students at the Renovaré Institute, speaking to them on learning the way of Christ through the mini mystics and inviting them into imaginative prayer and reflection.

I quickly rerouted my path, not wanting to make either of us uncomfortable. Their comment is one I contend with often. In our modern world, shaped by the age of information, science, and skepticism, we have forgotten the role imagination plays in truth and how we live it out.

I'm a science nerd. I subscribe to a daily email that summarizes discoveries in science. Facts, statistics, new discoveries—the ongoing revelation of the why and how of our living is end-lessly interesting to me. But I often wonder where imagination intersects with all this information.

Surely imagination fuels the process of hypothesizing, and cu-riosity is the fire for discovery itself. Imagination is also abso-lutely essential for possibility. We can study the facts, synthesize the statistics, and open our eyes to our surroundings to see that climate change is a danger. But unless we invite imagination to the table and feed her well, we will not find the way forward, and we will be left spinning our information into desolation.

We have grown blind to the ways that imagination already influ-ences adult living. When we worry about the future or ruminate on the past, we are imagining. The stories we tell ourselves about each other and about God contain a hearty dose of imagination. Remember that imagination takes the facts of any matter and helps us know what meaning to make and how to respond. Imagi-nation lives in the soul. In the place where mind, body, spirit, and social context unite to function—there imagination makes its bed. Love, joy, peace, patience, kindness, and gentleness all go to seed in the soul, planted by God and watered with imagination. When injustice, suffering, and sorrow find solace in the soul, God listens and then plants the kiss of imagination. Hope is born, and the peaceable kingdom inches forward.

IMAGINATIVE CREATIVITY:
MAKERS, DOERS, DREAMERS

Imagination also helps us live into the creative dimension of who we are. Creativity is the specialization of the Holy Spirit. Wasn't it the Spirit who hovered over the void, dreaming of what this world could be? Wasn't it the Spirit who burned like fire and blew like wind, bringing revelation and possibility for what this ancient new way of being might look like? If we want to experience the Spirit, we create. We cocreate spreadsheets and spanakopita. We cocreate community and crafts. We cocreate human beings (we all knew sex was going to weasel its way into this discussion) and homes. Listen, with the ear of your heart, to Dallas Willard's words from chapter three of *The Divine Conspiracy.*

> It is the "will" aspect of personal/spiritual reality that is its innermost core. In biblical language the will is usually referred to as "heart." It organizes all the dimensions of personal reality to form a life or a person. The will, or heart, is the executive center of the self. Thus, the center point of the spiritual in humans as well as in God is self-determination, also called freedom and creativity. Little children quickly learn to make things and to give them to those they love. If their souls are not crushed by life, as so many unfortunately are, they will continue to do this throughout their lives and at death will wish to leave to others the things they have produced or secured by their own efforts. Creative people in leadership (human affairs), in the arts, and in the realm of intellect are the most highly admired among us. Sometimes the creativity is a matter of steadfast faithfulness to ideals or relationships. We always place a tremendous premium on what comes from the center of our being, the heart.[1]

Creative imagination flows from the center of who we are. Imagination is how we use our minds to engage and change the world. It helps us to harness and bring into actuality human freedom and flexibility.

In a delightful little Pendle Hill pamphlet titled *God's Invitation to Creative Play*, Jesse White writes about common creative fears that keep us from joining God in artistic expression.[2] If any of these fears resonate with you, try some of the following welcoming practices.

If I make art, it will be ugly: practice intentionally making ugly art. Ask the Spirit to show you how.

If I make a mistake, I will lose my credibility: engage with Renovaré's "Art + Faith" webinar.[3] Follow a few of the links and try some of the recommendations.

My creativity isn't as good as someone else's creativity: begin by making something . . . dinner, a drawing, a marketing plan, a floral arrangement, a poem, a piece of music. Then return to your altar, the one with the cute picture of yourself as a child. Become aware of God, our Divine Parent. Show God your creation, telling God about the process, giving God access to this part of who you are. Then listen. Be still and listen to God's response.

WONDERMENT IS NOT CHEWING GUM

The lifeblood of creativity is wonder. John O'Donohue writes, "One of the reasons that we wonder is because we are limited, and that limitation is one of the great gateways of wonder."[4] It makes sense, then, that children are stupendous wonderers. They are born limited in just about every way. As we age and start to know a bit about this world of ours, as we bear the woundedness of soul and body, the gift of wonder can lessen or, tragically, cease altogether. The world grows small and predictable. Our desire to control and avoid pain offers a security that is essentially false. It hems us in and hems wonder out.

One summer day, I sent my young children outside to play, accompanied by our red heeler dog Sage. Sage was as good as her name. While she was trained to round up cattle and sheep, she was an expert with children. Wiser than her years and tender with puppy affection, she stayed near to them, gladly playing in whatever way they would let her while continually circling, keeping them nearby.

Every parent knows the feeling of unexpected silence. It descends on parental ears first as freedom, then as fear. I was on the other side of the house, hanging out a week's worth of laundry. Just after clothespinning the last item, I noticed the lack of sound or movement from where the kids were. First, the freedom made room for some of my own thoughts; then, fear shocked my system into a dead run in their direction. We live in area that is known for bears and mountain lions; my imagination did its worst. As I rounded the corner, an ice-cold stream of water hit my face with force.

Anwen let out a loud cackle laced with sinister delight. My body and mind tried to make sense of what was before me. One child, water weapon in hand, was covered head to toe in mud. Another was squatting near a newly made mud hole—who knows how deep—filled with muddy water. Aidan was only partially covered in mud and was carefully crafting treasures with whatever was excavated.

"Look at what we're making!" Aidan said.

"Oh, I see," I said, wiping the water from my face and breathing deeply—trying to backpedal the heart attack I was having.

"Want some lunch?" Aidan asked, and filled a little clay bowl with water and offered it to Sage, who dutifully lapped it up, mud and all.

"Mama, want some lunch?" Anwen asked, mimicking Aidan, but louder, maybe thinking my hearing had been sprayed away by the water hose.

"Sure," I answered, but sat down on a rock out of the mud and away from the water hose.

"Lunch is over here," Aidan told me, pointing to a spot where mud creations were drying in the sun.

"What if I eat lunch from over here?" I asked.

"Don't worry, Mom," Aidan said, "if you don't want to get your clothes dirty, you can take them off like Anwen has." It was at that point I realized that while Anwen was covered in mud, she wasn't covered in clothing.

I wish I could say that on that day, I rolled up my pant legs and accepted the invitation to lunch. But I didn't. My pressing to-do list and my resistance to do something that seemed to serve no purpose kept me from going all in. My capacity for wonder withered. I sat on the rock a little longer, but eventually went back to work. I was glad that my children were playing, but I had forgotten how to partake in the earthy mysticism of imagining.

THE CREATIVE PERMEABILITY OF PLAY AND WORK

For many of us, work is made of "have-tos" brought on by the shared experience of scarcity. In order to make ends meet, people have to work.

For my family of origin, life is work and work is life. If we were going to play, we did it at work, and if we were going to create, we also did it at work. I learned to tell my first jokes at my grandparents' deli at the tender age of four while counting out change to customers. Standing on the chest freezer full of frozen fries and chicken strips, I imagined that I was a standup comedian, helping people to laugh when life was tough. It was fun to stack the soda cans in such a way that they mimicked the colors of the rainbow, and I wrote my first book on brown paper bags cut and glued together.

Some twenty years later, I grabbed a hot plate of scrambled eggs, hash browns, and toast from under the warmer. Waiting tables at my grandparents' diner in Colorado City, Texas (same grandparents, different business), was good, paying work in the summers between my college years. As I bolted out of the swinging doors, arms loaded with hot plates and a coffee pot, I realized that table twelve didn't want hash browns—something about being allergic to potatoes. So I turned on my heel and said to my grandfather, who was working the grill frying bacon and eggs, "They don't want hash browns. Can you take them off?" He gave me the kind of look that said, "Who in their right mind doesn't like potatoes?"

Still, he scraped the eggs and toast onto a clean plate and sent me out and that was that. The next day we were working the morning shift together again. It was a busy morning, and a rush of oil field workers filled the diner, four to a table, with muddy boots and weathered faces. After topping off coffee cups (all fully caffeinated—no decaf with this bunch), I rushed to the kitchen, filled my arms with hot plates, and then noticed that there were no hash browns on these plates. Four plates lined up on my arm (which requires creativity and a bit of circus aptitude), and not one of them had hash browns.

"Uh, Papa, where's the hash browns?"

With an eye roll and a smirky grin he said, "You didn't want them yesterday. Why would you want them today?"

With all the tenderness and patience I could muster at five a.m., I returned the eye roll and said, "Very funny. Different people. Different potato preference."

He had a big batch cooking in one corner of the grill, which was arranged like a work of art. I walked over, and he distributed the goods on the plates—flinging potato parts all over the place as he did so.

Everyone got the breakfast they had ordered that morning, and I remembered the cheeky encounter throughout the day as I fished potato bits out of my apron pockets. Today, we still ask each other, "Do you want hash browns with that?" Our creative work together connected us, and the play continues.

Reflecting on this day working with Papa, it was the simple difference of potato preferences that made the way for play and imagination. I wonder if imitation and imagination might be a distinction between work that is life giving and work that is life draining. Even in food service, people tend to lean toward sameness; the ubiquity of chain restaurants and factory-produced foods tells us that. Our driving need for security and safety limp us toward what is an imitation of an original creation. Imitation might be the first step in a creative endeavor, but if we are to follow in the way of our Creator, imagination must be the second step. For work to be life giving, we must have space to use our imaginations to lapse in play and go from imitating to cocreating.

Work is not the opposite of creativity and play. Work is a place to funnel our creativity through play. I've learned this from a friend who is an accountant and finds incredible joy and imagination in creating spreadsheets. She just lights up when creatively working with categories, numbers, and systems.

Children know the thrill of cocreating with God. Using their imagination and any old thing they can find, they create cargo ships, castles, cars, or whatever else may wander into their imaginative threshold. In acts of creation, children and adults lose themselves and connect with the Creator who invites them into an adventure beyond themselves.

Imagination is essential to faith. We will not trust an unseen God without a little imagination, and we will not be able to catch a vision of the kingdom of God or participate in it without imagination. Imagination isn't dabbling in what isn't real; instead, it helps us to live with what is unseen. Faith, hope, and love are all made tangible by imagination.

Welcoming Practices

Imagine Scripture. Engage imaginatively with the story of Jesus and the little children in Mark 10:13-16. Set aside three days to engage with this passage of Scripture. Follow the six steps each day, using the Day 1, Day 2, or Day 3 focus. Create a response after each day's encounter. The response could be a journal entry, art expression, or sharing what you discovered with a friend. Here's a brief intro to reading with your imagination:

First, take two minutes before reading to center your heart, mind, and body.

Second, invite the Spirit to speak to you through your imagination.

Third, read the passage through once. Get the general picture of the passage. Who is present; where is the story occurring; what is happening?

Fourth, read the passage again; this time, imagine that you are present. Where are you? Who are you? What do you see? What do you smell? What do you hear? What do you taste? What do you touch?

Fifth, stay in the passage. Let your imagination guide you in and through this passage.

Sixth, what does the Spirit want you to know or experience? As Saint Benedict writes in the prologue to his rule, "Attend with the ear of your heart."[5]

Day 1: Imagine that you are one of the people who are bringing children to Jesus. Ask yourself, "What is my motive for bringing the children?" Enter into a conversation with Jesus about your motive.

Day 2: Imagine that you are one of the disciples who spoke sternly to the children. Ask yourself, "Why did I speak sternly? How does the presence of children change this setting?" Enter into a conversation with Jesus about the changes that children bring.

Day 3: Imagine that you are one of the children. Ask yourself, "How does it feel to be brought to Jesus?" "What do I feel like doing when I hear the disciples speak sternly about my presence?" Last, feel the touch of Jesus on your body, and hear him use his words to defend you. Smell his breath; touch his face; talk with him.

Play with problems. Is there a circumstance, event, or person in your life that feels like a roadblock? An encounter with someone that continues to circle in your mind before you sleep or when you are doing mundane tasks? Next time this happens, shift your focus to the Spirit and ask for help, perhaps something like, "Holy Spirit, open my imagination to solutions that I can't see." Then engage your imagination. Imagine the situation in your mind; drawing it on paper can help. (Stick figures are completely acceptable.) Be sure to include the Spirit in your drawing. Watch the situation like you are watching a movie from your couch. Play out the most ridiculous and funny solution possible. Embrace the fullness of the absurd, let it fill the space. Then watch it again, this time let your inner pessimist run the show. What would be the worst-case scenario? Let your shadow side and fear come into the light. Be sure to see the Spirit in the scene. What is the Spirit doing? Last, see yourself sitting with the Spirit and ask what your next faithful step is. What is the one thing you are to do next?

Learn from a book. Children's picture books are built on imagination! So, a reading list on the topic of imagination could be oh-so-long. Still, here are a few to get you started: *Maybe: A Story About the Endless Potential in All of Us* by Kobi Yamada and Gabriella Barouch; *Will's Mammoth* by Rafe Martin and Stephen Gammel. I have often asked children to write their own words for the illustrations in *Will's Mammoth;* give it a try. After engaging with these suggestions, wander into the children's area at your local bookstore and follow your curiosity. Sit on the floor or in the tiny chairs and lose track of time and yourself in story. You might find a child near to you wondering what you're doing. Feel free to read aloud to them; it will be life changing.

8

Humor and the Holy Fool

*The child laughs because he has not yet been brainwashed
and thereby blinded to the truly amusing.*

ELTON TRUEBLOOD

It was the conversation that had to happen. We needed to tell
our children about my upcoming surgeries—mastectomy and
oophorectomy—without scaring them to death. I wanted to
prepare them, but I didn't want them to feel responsible for
making things better. I didn't want them to worry, but I did want
them to know things could get messy.

We met around the kitchen table, the center of life in our home,
a common, earthy place where we share meals, games and craft
projects, and school. Giant windows on two sides keep nature near
but not intrusive; the fireplace on the other side is our only source
of heat, a reminder of inner and outer warmth. With clear medical
language and a calm steady tone, my husband, Doug, explained to
them what the BRCA2 gene mutation meant.

Clear, concise medical explanations were not unusual for
our family. I remember one conversation and the subsequent

questions around why the rooster jumped on the back of the chickens, and why it wasn't necessarily helping the chickens to whack the rooster with a stick. With precise vocabulary, Doug had waded into the waters of chicken reproduction. A few years later, when the children were just entering their teenage years, we brought home a male goat for our four females. Doug discreetly and calmly explained that the mating ritual of the male goat, which included peeing in his own beard, was not the mating ritual of human beings—and further, that if they ever met a young man who tried that particular circus trick, they were to run as fast as possible in the opposite direction.

I felt certain that we had laid the foundation for difficult conversations. Doug began with the facts about DNA, and then I took over, explaining that the removal of my ovaries would cause big changes in my hormones and therefore in my feelings. Over time I would learn to navigate those feelings, but at first it might be a little rough; I might get sad or angry, but it would not be at or about them. In the middle of my overexplaining and hypersensitivity, Anwen, only eleven years old at the time, dropped her head to the table with a sudden thud. We all stopped and stared. She lifted it in the most dramatic fashion and spouted off, her words dripping with sarcasm: "Oh, great. I guess we'll learn some new swear words."

The shocking absurdity of her statement in the middle of what we were facing moved us to silence. Then we all burst into laughter, that kind of laughter that is so deeply cleansing it brings you to tears. Who was she kidding? Since I come from the West Texas oil fields, she had already heard all the swear words there were to learn. In fact, when Doug and I first married I tried to curb my flowing sailor's tongue by placing a dollar bill in a glass jar for every profanity uttered. We bought our first home with that money, and the earthy habit has never entirely left me.

THE GIFT OF LAUGHTER

Laughter can be a gift in a difficult time. Where sorrow, fear, pain, and loss suck the oxygen out of the room, laughter opens up the windows. Laughter is a masterful tool of the Holy Spirit, who blows in unexpectedly, bringing light and sacred perspective where there is little. Humor is the humus of our human existence. Humor is a response to life's leftovers and cataclysmic mistakes, that which isn't neat or tidy, but can be transformed into life giving clarity and connection. It is the reminder to take ourselves lightly, that while we might be holy, we are only holy fools at best.

Jesuit priest and writer James Martin calls humor "an essential but neglected requirement of spirituality."[1] He has written a hilarious and surprisingly informative book on humor and the spiritual life, *Between Heaven and Mirth*. Martin takes his readers through a serious study of joy, both the divine and human variety. He doesn't slink from the pain and sorrow of life but invites us to a whole human experience by embracing the humor within it all.

I don't know about you, but my experiences in church have been devoid of intentional humor. There were many sermons about the seriousness of following Christ, sermons about the dangers of hell, warnings about behavior that might lead to debauchery, but I've never heard a sermon on the humor of Christ or his friends. I have wondered if in our efforts to take the way of Christ seriously, pride snuck in and humor along with humility left the building. We mistakenly thought that the serious call to a devout and holy life couldn't coexist with holy fools and mad hatters, but we were wrong. Saint Teresa of Ávila is famously quoted as saying, "A sad nun is a bad nun. I am more afraid of one unhappy sister than a crowd of evil spirits."[2] Talk about a superb use of hyperbole, humor's master tool! Saint Teresa is not calling humorless nuns bad. But she is pointing out that without humor, we aren't whole, we aren't seeing correctly. When our sight is whole, then we see, as Christ sees, that there's quite a bit of absurdity in this world.

Humor puts the kibosh on arrogance, pretense, and even fear. It brings our high-flying ideals back down to earth where they can live within humanity. Quaker professor Howard Macy says, "Humor actually has a lot to do with how we understand ourselves, how we see the world, how we relate effectively with others, and ultimately, how we come to glad wholeness in our lives."[3] From this perspective, Anwen was the most holy among us! Somehow (hello, Holy Spirit) she understood that none of us were actually in danger. Whatever circumstance we were in, God would be with us and therefore we were safe. Safety doesn't mean that terrible, horrible, no good, very bad things don't happen; it means that we are never alone in them. As the Beatitudes remind us, ultimately, our blessedness is determined by God's presence with us. And Jesus' name, Emmanuel, reveals that God is always with us. Anwen's perfectly timed gift of laughter reminded my family of the truth of our smallness and God's promise of presence.

CHILDREN AND HUMOR

Children laugh more than adults. That much is agreed upon, but *how* much more they laugh is hard to determine. Laughter serves a utilitarian purpose for children as a means to gain much-needed attention and connection from the adults that assure their survival. A baby's first laugh is a moment of great celebration in a family. Shared laughter is responsive, bonding, and supplies a dopamine hit for all within earshot. It is real evidence of the give and take of love. The parents have set their will to keeping this little human alive, and the child's laughter is a peal of shared gratitude. From the infant's humble state connection flows.

A recent study of Swedish preschools reveals that we all laugh more when we are with others.[4] Humor helps us to connect with one another. Thus, children laugh more when they are with other children and adults laugh more when with other adults. The homogeneous selection seems to be connected to how each person welcomes difference. The study showed that the more open-hearted we are of those who are different from us, be it age, gender, or something else, the more we laugh. In this way, humor flows from cultivated curiosity and wonderment. Through laughter, difference finds connection.

Children not only laugh for connection, but they also laugh out of sheer delight and surprise. (Just Google children laughing with dogs, and you'll find a long list of videos that will make your day.) I learned this little lesson from a group of fourth graders in New York.

Ashley had been standing so long at my desk that I finally pulled up a chair for her. Together, we worked on the division process for what felt like hours. "I just don't get it, miss," she wailed. We had gone as far as she could go that afternoon. Fourth grade is full of big jumps, academically, socially, and physically. Being gentle was, sadly, a rare grace in my early teaching years, but I was learning.

I plunked my own arm down in mutual frustration and quickly noticed something stuck to it—a small, balled-up piece of glue. Earlier that day we'd been working on an art project, and clearly things had gotten out of hand. An idea came to me, and somehow I had just enough of my inner fourth grader present to run with it.

"Hey, Ashley," I said, "see this little piece of glue? I'm going to stick it on my face right under my nose, so it looks like a booger."

At first, she looked at me with shock. But then she started to laugh. "No, no. Let me," she returned. "I'll go back to my small group with it on my face and we can see who laughs first!" We were in the joke together as she stuck the glue just under her nose and wandered back to her cooperative learning group. All the members glanced at her; most didn't notice the glue, but went back to their math problems. But Ashley's best friend noticed and immediately began trying to signal a solution. Ashley feigned ignorance and started conversations with the kids in her group. With each new look, a smile and a snicker emerged. After a few minutes of dialogue, Ashley landed the finale of her little performance by pulling the fake booger off her face and popping it in her mouth. We both fell to the floor cackling while the members of her group tried to decide whether they should laugh or barf.

We needed that breath of fresh air to remember our humanity, to remember to take ourselves and our limitations lightly. We needed something brimming with delight and surprise, something that would remind us that we were on the same side in the mathematics struggle. Humor was just the thing.

THE SHAPE OF HUMOR

There are many kinds and colors of humor. Many of us have been on the harmful side of humor, the kind that alienates and separates. This kind of humor that brings about shame rather than joy isn't from God and is in no way good. But sacred, holy humor brings people together, and produces the fruits of the Spirit such as peace, joy, patience, kindness, gentleness, and radical good will. That is not to say that humor isn't a powerful tool that reveals truth. (We'll get to that a bit later.) Holy humor is not superficial, but contains a profound truth, something real that is unseen.

Quaker Elton Trueblood reminds us that "mirth and compassion are compatible."[5] We need not turn on one another to enjoy the benefits of humor; however, even that kind of humor reveals truth about the one using it. We human beings are a wounded lot, and we can use humor to try and make others feel smaller, less significant, which reveals our own true poverty of soul. Trueblood goes on to remind us that humor and suffering are often expressions of deep pain. The weaving together of these seeming opposites can be a grace in dark times. Humor is not denying pain, but revealing a deeper attachment to God, who is within it and beyond it.

Much of adult laughter comes from noticing the absurd— sitcoms are pudding proof. But we don't have to watch sitcoms to engage with absurdity; standup comedy will do just fine. Jim Gaffigan's comedy is anchored in calling out the absurd in our world. If you need a good laugh at our absurdities, you can see him on YouTube: "Best CATHOLIC Jokes Compilation" is hilarious, and I'm not even Catholic.[6] Noticing the incongruences of Western living and then wrapping them in humor has the potential to open our eyes and set us free from the bondage of phony exceptionalism.

At around eight or nine years old, children begin to tinker with telling jokes. For the listening adult, they are often hilariously unfunny. They can lack a punch line, or, for that matter, irony of any kind. Researchers tell us that we need three things for this kind of humor: imagination, language, and the ability to take a different perspective.[7] Children are experts in imagination, but language and social awareness take time to develop. That's why putting underpants on one's head and running around the neighborhood is the pinnacle of hilarity to a five-year-old. At this stage, imagination is engaged, but language and social awareness are still growing. One of the great delights of children in this age range is to discover the joke book section in the library.

Curiously, this is also the time in their lives when children are working through which of their fears are real and which are unfounded. In practicing their joke-telling skills, they cultivate a playful sense around what is safe. When their sense of safety is grounded in God's love, they can use humor to drain the power from what frightens them.

Engagement with paradox can give rise to the comic element. When we piddle around with paradox, we nod to our limited capacity for understanding. God being three and one is a biggie. We try to put words around something our rational minds just can't grasp. A surprising array of theologians have tried to squeeze the Trinity into analogies: shamrocks, eggs, three states of water, ice cream, and even fidget spinners. We, adults, are shockingly blind to the limits of our knowledge and wisdom.

HUMOR, HUMILITY, AND POWER

Humor and humility go hand in hand. To catch a glimpse of humility, we need only to look at God. In the first three chapters of Genesis, we begin to get to know this God who chooses humility. God empowers human persons, giving them the agency to use their power in the service of their own knowledge, their own needs, and even their own wounds. This empowering of another is a sacred characteristic of God. God radiates humility by honoring the will of human beings. In an act of holy self-differentiation, God not only empowers and encourages, but in fact requires human power sharing as a means of relationship. Rather than ruling human beings, God cultivates relationship by offering power through choice.

We can also look at the life of Jesus. The incarnation is an act of God's self-emptying to accompany human beings. Jesus embodies a humility that is necessary to rightly ordered power dynamics. We can wander through the Gospels and see how Jesus exudes humility by shifting power to the person in front of him. In encounter after encounter, Jesus embodies humility by giving attention to those who were on the margins of society with little power of their own. He offered invitation rather than manipulating or seeking to control. And he honored both their freedom to step in the direction of the invitation and their freedom to walk away. Human will, it seems, is God's folly. Elizabeth-Anne Stewart, spiritual director, life coach, and author, writes, "How wise of God to expand our hearts through the trials and joys of our lives. How wise of our God to love us into choosing to love God. God had two options: to choose tyranny or foolishness—how wise of God to choose folly."[8]

Humility is an elusive human characteristic. Despite many definitions, we struggle to understand and embody it. Dallas Willard gives us a glimpse of what humility might look like: a person who embodies humility never pushes, never presumes, and never pretends.[9] Attention to these three *p*'s of humility can help us notice when we are living from a disordered relationship with power. Not every instance of pushing, presuming, or pretending is of disordered power, but each is an instance where we are invited to check in with our motives and where we see power flowing. To be sure, like attuning to presence, the ordering and disordering of power happens in an instant.

Desmond Tutu and the Dalai Lama teach about and embody lives of humility in their *Book of Joy*. Although the Dalai Lama is the political and religious leader of the Tibetan people, he considers himself "just one human being out of seven billion."[10] His wider perspective can help us to understand our place in the cosmos. Desmond Tutu, a South African bishop and theologian who fought against apartheid and for human rights, said of himself that "he loved, he laughed, he cried."[11] Disordered power thrives in the pinholes of limited scope. To be a big fish in a little pond is an ego boost; but to realize that the little pond is actually an inlet for an enormous ocean humbles us.

Sister Joan Chittister reminds us that humility is not about humiliation. Instead it is:

> about understanding and realizing the truth of the self. It is how we see ourselves that determines how we respond to others that determines how we fare and what we become in the human community. And it is humility that stands to set us free. Free from the ambition that drives us, from the angers that rule us, from the greed that consumes us, from the chains we have mistaken for success and superiority.[12]

Desmond Tutu used humor, specifically what he called "self-denigrating humor," to diffuse tense situations that were filled with heightened emotions ready to blow. His own cultivated humility gave him access to this powerful tool. He knew in the very cells of his body that he was of great worth as a beloved of God, and so was freed from the ego need to self-inflate. Desmond Tutu cultivated the gift of seeing the absurd, naming it, and then laughing his way to freedom. He learned to take himself lightly, to embrace the posture of holy fool.

HOLY FOOLERY

One thing that I notice when reading about saints, desert fathers and mothers, elders, exemplars, and wisdom teachers of our faith is the thread of holy foolery woven throughout their lives. In Jon Sweeney's book *The St. Francis Holy Fool Prayer Book,* he tells four stories of Brother Juniper, who went naked to town, cooked a whole chicken (feathers and everything) for friars, played on a seesaw in Rome, and became rapt with ecstasy one day at Mass.[13] (Makes chewing gum during the Eucharist seem small in comparison.) In each of these stories, Brother Juniper is cultivating humility and, perhaps unbeknownst to him, calling the community to truth. Saint Francis, Brother Juniper, and others like them engage in a playful, humorous, humility that helped them to take themselves less seriously. As Trueblood wrote, "Laughter can, if taken aright, have a purgative effect.... Humor is redemptive when it leads to comic self-discovery."[14]

Holy fools are governed by the generous boundaries of the kingdom of God, which often come in conflict with our culture, whether secular or religious. Holy fools live at the edges of society with the marginalized. They share in the suffering, loneliness, and isolation. They are generally careless with institutions of power or prestige. Whether through innocence or cultivated character, they live the words of Julia Roberts in the movie *Steel Magnolias:* "An ounce of pretension is worth a pound of manure."[15] They are neither center right nor center left, but centered within Christ. With arms wide open, strangely reminiscent of the cross, they simply can't be boxed in to political or religious constructs.

Desmond Tutu is a wonderful example of holy foolishness. If you watch the short film *Mission Joy: Finding Happiness in Troubled Times,* you will hear his laughter, playfulness, and his prophetic bent. Tutu was a deeply prayerful human being; the roots of his trust in God's loving presence went deep. It was this depth in Christ that helped him to see the goodness in all of humanity, to take himself lightly, and to speak truth to power. He practiced what he preached, chairing the Truth and Reconciliation Committee and advocating for compassionate response.[16]

Like humor, there are various kinds of fools. Holy fools don't live from the place of spectacle. What they say or do doesn't come from an egotistical need to be seen or heard. In our world today, we have become compulsively attached to this desire. We are living at the mercy of our unmet desire to belong. Creating rebellious spectacle for spectacle's sake is not the way of the holy fool; however, inviting honest reflection is. For the holy fool, attention given them is not absorbed but reflected back. It is a means to deeper listening and deeper engagement. Holy fools are never fools for the compulsive self, but fools for God and others. Holy foolery never flows from malice, but love. Love can look like disobedience, says Father Edward Hays in his book *Mad Hatters: A Handbook for Hobbyhorse Holiness.*[17]

Three types of disobedience that holy fools can be called to are: nonviolent civil disobedience, social-family disobedience, and sacred disobedience. Each require a faithful discernment before engaging. Children are notoriously disobedient and we as parents can be blind to the gift of their disobedience. (Seriously, read that sentence again, it took me hours to gather the courage to write it.) Disobedience is revelatory. It took me much too long to learn that when my children disobeyed it was a whisper from the Spirit, saying, "Find out why, and reflect on it." When I followed the Spirit's lead, I often learned something tender and hidden about my children or myself. I learned about my own wounds and how I might be shackling my children with them. I learned about my children and their deep desires and frustrations. I learned changing the rules, asking forgiveness, or extending grace isn't weak parenting, but connected parenting—and that's good for everyone.

Holy foolishness is divine wisdom. You will know it by its generosity and love. You will know it by its vulnerability. The dance of the holy fool has two steps: truth and gentleness. Humans struggle to hear truth. We are prone to distraction and denial. Our blessed ego wants only the truth that serves it. The holy fool can use humor to sidestep our frozen pronation, leading us into the truth that will set us free to dance.

Holy foolery is needed in times of transition. And we, dear siblings, are in transition. It is holy foolery that can help us to see our disordered attachments, where we have not loved God, our neighbor, or ourselves well. Through holy foolery, we begin to see what needs to be left behind as we move toward something new.

ON BEING A WINDBAG

The word *fool* comes from the Latin *follis,* meaning bag of wind. The West Texas wind is wild; it sweeps the land clear, shaping and shifting sand and seed. On windy days, I would tie a string to a plastic sack to make a kite. I'd stand all day in the empty lot next door holding on to the string waiting and watching for that bag to catch what I couldn't see but knew was there. Christians are essentially windbags.

This word *windbag*, which could be denigrating, is spot on when we are talking about holy fools. We are containers for the wind of the Spirit; we catch and are propelled by what the Spirit is doing in this wide and wonderful world. Holy fools are honest enough to know that they know very little of what the Spirit is up to, but they are flexible and willing enough to cooperate and go where it will.

To be sure, we are all fools; the difference is cultivating the holy foolishness within. In her book *Jesus the Holy Fool,* Stewart reminds us that we need both fools and sages. The wisest sage knows and admits the limits of their capability and wisdom even as they play their way through life. She writes, "Holy Foolishness is a response to life which is playful, joyful, outrageous at times, authentic, inclusive, prophetic, countercultural, naive, uninhibited, transformational, spontaneous, passionate and daring."[18]

Welcoming Practices

Awaken to death. There was a time in the not-so-distant past when we were foolish enough to call death's bluff on a daily basis. Holy fools decorated with skulls and crosses, instruments of death (how about hanging a lovely wood carving of a guillotine on your living room wall?). What if the picture of the Laughing Jesus (Google it) is an illustration of Jesus just after resurrection? Maybe he did throw his head back and say, "Whoopee, it worked!" Christianity is unique in that one of our major symbols is one of death; it is our holy foolishness that turns its nose up at death and says, "You will not have the last word." We live in cycles of death daily: dying to self, dying to live, dying to sin and our disordered attachments. Death is part of living and we might as well welcome it to the table. So, channel your inner biker and move a skull into your living space. (Note to my beloved family: a mounted animal head on the wall does not count.) Let it remind you of your death, and moreover, that death does not have the last word. Or you could place a picture of the Laughing Jesus in your living space. Practice laughing with Jesus, rejoicing over the moments of resurrection dotted within your life. Christian recording artist Carolyn Arends has a super fun song on her album *Recognition* titled "Memento Mori," which is Latin for "Remember you will die." It's quite catchy, and the lyrics are both funny and deeply true.

Try a smiling meditation. Many of us have practiced meditation and centering prayer for years, and our faces show it. And some of us have been gifted with a resting face that looks, shall we say, less than happy. Try letting your body lead your meditation time. While meditating or practicing centering prayer, turn the corners of your mouth up into a smile. Allow your body to lead you into contemplating God as the most joyous being in the universe. Notice what this stirs in you.

Learn from a book. Read *Advice to Little Girls* by Mark Twain and pictures by Vladimir Radunsky. This outrageous little book found me in Powell's Bookstore in Portland, where I laughed so loudly that my children abandoned me on site. The classic *Alexander and the Terrible, No Good, Very Bad Day* by Judith Viorst should be standard reading for all politicians and priests. Last, *The Three Questions* by Jon J. Muth (based on a story by Tolstoy) is a visual and, when read aloud, auditory experience into sacred reflection. It will sharpen your seeing and hearing.

9

Freedom to Learn

Is life not full of opportunities for learning love? Every man and woman every day has a thousand of them. The world is not a playground; it is a schoolroom. Life is not a holiday, but an education. And the one eternal lesson for us all is how better we can love.

HENRY DRUMMOND

In an interview on the podcast *The Takeaway*, Rachel Wu, an assistant professor of psychology at the University of California, speaks of the benefits of the learner mindset for older adults.[1] We assume that adults struggle more to learn new things, but in reality, it's hard for all of us. Children, though, have some distinct advantages.

Toddlers and young children arguably show the most visible progress for learning. During these years, they learn that they have bodies and how their bodies work. They learn that there are other bodies in the world and how to get along with the other bodies. They learn to communicate; they learn physics and biology.

Once while trying to wrangle my two-year-old into her car seat, I heard a woman the next car over exclaim to her offspring, "For the love of all that's holy, son, don't lick the wheel wells of the car!" Children are constantly learning.

If they are within a safe community, children will learn that their needs will be met. The experiential knowledge that their needs are met frees them to pursue the other objects of their curiosity. With this freedom, they may become enamored with words and pictures and learn to read. With this freedom, they may experiment with dirt and water and learn the various physical states of matter. When children are not concerned with their safety, they are free to listen to the spirit of curiosity and follow.

This is true in our spiritual life as well. Earlier, we explored the idea of attaching to God, our Divine Parent. When our picture of God is one where God can be trusted and we are held safe in God's tender loving care, we will be free even to learn. If our sense of belonging is held by God, our survival will not be shaken. Following our spiritual curiosity helps us to get to know God on a level that is beyond dogma, creed, or even biblical inerrancy. It leads us to experiential knowing, which deepens trust.

FREE TO FAIL

Each week I have the incredible opportunity to meet with adults and children in spiritual direction. While I am the (clears throat) director, there's little directing on my part. Mostly I sit tight and marvel at what God is up to in the life of another. One day, while I was marveling my socks off, a directee quoted Yoda—yeah, that Yoda. "Pass on what you have learned. Strength, mastery, hmm . . . but weakness, folly, failure also. Yes, failure most of all. Luke, we are what they grow beyond. That is the burden of all masters."[2]

A child who is learning to walk will fall thousands of times. Failure is part of the learning. We don't fault a child as they learn to eat; in fact, we take pictures instead. Blueberries and chocolate cake strung from highchair to low wall—we expect this chaos as kids learn to get the spoon from the plate to their mouths. But we adults see failure as a final mark of our efforts, rather than as part of the process. Our preoccupation with outcomes can become a compulsion. We can become so debilitated by perfectionism that we alienate ourselves from all risk and even joy. In our walk with God, failure offers us many gifts. Perfection doesn't prepare; presence does. There is no learning without failure. What we understand about ourselves, God, and even others will always be a mystery. When we experience failure, we come up against that mystery. We are invited to remember that the depths cannot be plumbed or tamed.

Parenting failure has been the hardest pill to choke down for me. My children couldn't have been more than four and seven years old when I gathered them both on the couch in the living room. I was just on the other side of a conversation with Jesus about how I disciplined. After a ton of reflection, prayer, and repentance, I could see that spanking my kids was not in anyone's best interest. So, I told them that, and I asked their forgiveness. My tears were evidence of my deep regret, and in the way of Christ and children, they forgave wholeheartedly.

In Luke 8:40-56, the fear of death and the fear of shame—two huge parenting fears—emerge. At the beginning, we meet a father bent low with love and anguish for his dying daughter. She was his only daughter, and his love for her threw him at Jesus' feet. He was humbled to the point of begging for help for her very life. Love does that. Love for our children places us in the most vulnerable of positions. If we allow ourselves to come close to our children, to connect with them on the deepest level, it will cost us. Our pride, our tightly held ideas and ideals, our lofty plans for the future, and sense of security will be burned away by Love. Parenting is a unique learning school for love. We get a visceral picture in the pleading of this father for his daughter. How has your love for children (even your own childhood self) bent you low?

In the second story, we see the ongoing destruction caused by shame. The woman in the story had been bent low not only by her disease, but also by the religious and cultural shame surrounding her gender and the symptoms of her disease. Bleeding. The passage says she had been "suffering from hemorrhages for twelve years" (Luke 8:43). Her unending wounds were literally the thing she could never talk about. Her shame kept her isolated and hidden—a fate worse than the wounds themselves.

Parental shame is a real wound, and it festers and weeps as we attempt to shut it off and shove it down deeper into our souls. I have sat with parents who suffer in silence and isolation, bent low by parenting shame. Whether our shame comes from our acts as parents or the actions of our children, the weight of shame is heavy. How has parental shame touched your life?

Fear of death and fear of shame numb our connection with God, with ourselves, and with others, especially the children in our lives. In Luke 8, we see that both Jairus and the woman healed experienced the grace and healing of Jesus when they let themselves feel and moved closer. They risked it all to draw near to the One they hoped could heal their fears. When in the midst of our fears we draw near to Christ, we will hear him call us by name. With gentleness, he invites us and our fears out of hiding, saying, "Do not fear. You can trust me. You can trust me with your children. You can trust me with your shame."

LEARNING IS CONNECTED TO LIVING

A child's number one mandate is to learn. Humor, play, and imagination all serve our learning. When children blow bubbles in the bathtub, they are learning. When they grab the cat's tail, they are learning. When they scream their protest at your constant re-routing away from the Christmas tree, they are learning. We begin as learning creatures, and we continue as learning creatures throughout our lives. In his book *Beginners,* Tom Vanderbilt tells of his adventures trying to learn chess, singing, surfing, drawing, and juggling.[3] He chose these skills specifically because they wouldn't enhance his résumé and he knew mastery of them was impossible. In the learning, he discovered joy and connection.

I wonder if Jesus held children up as an example because of their natural learning mindset. Children are able to learn because they possess the humility of knowing that they don't know. They hold their knowledge lightly, which keeps curiosity hot within them.

In the podcast I mentioned at the start of the chapter, Wu notes that children have an advantage in learning because they are surrounded by a helping community. They are almost always near someone who can help them follow their curiosity and find their answers. When young children are learning to speak, adults are around talking with them and helping them find their own expression. These helpers, ready to respond when called upon, characterize the best learning environments for children and adults.

But of course, as adults, we can find asking for help both humbling and humiliating. As we've grown, we have somehow committed to a scarcity model of knowledge—like there isn't enough for everyone and so asking for help from another is threatening.

We forget what children know. Knowledge is for everyone, and, as our community learns together, we grow together. Once, a parent who was a new Christian reached out to me, worried about raising their child in the way of Jesus while being so new to their own relationship with Christ. "What a wonderful opportunity," I responded. "As you learn together, you will grow together." Learning together connects us at an experiential level.

CURIOSITY AND CONNECTION

The Black Canyon of the Gunnison is a national park in our neck of the woods. When my daughters were young, we would drive the steep windy road to the bottom of the park, station our car next to the Gunnison River, and camp. I loved the sound of the rushing water and the unmistakable sense of smallness that comes from peering up at more than two thousand feet of sheer rock face.

The Black Canyon gets its name from the mere thirty-three minutes of sunlight a day afforded to the bottom. It's a welcome respite to the high-altitude, intense sun that we receive year-round, especially in summer. At the bottom, the Gunnison River is crystal clear, with little dirt or detritus to muddy the waters. Wandering along its rocky banks and discovering stony and weedy treasures is an excellent way to follow curiosity.

On one trip my dad went with us. He's a no-nonsense Vietnam vet shaped by struggle and humbled by his extravagant love for his granddaughters. One afternoon, while I napped with Anwen, he and Aidan went for a walk.

Aidan entered the world with a love for learning. At five years old, she gobbled up any information offered to her. She learned to honor her bent toward curiosity through active wondering. Naturally a quiet child, Aidan learned to speak later than her peers.

Only after careful consideration of her words and hours of pondering would she, with freedom, offer her conclusions. I heard a bit of their conversation as they wandered and wondered toward the river.

"Grand," Aidan said, "did you know that there is an asteroid belt between the inner and outer planets?"

"No kidding?" replied Dad matter-of-factly as he looked up at the canyon walls and into the sky. He took every word she spoke as gospel truth.

"Yeah, there is. These big rocks probably come from there," she said, pointing at the mammoth boulders that dotted the canyon floor.

"You're smarter than I am, so it must be," he said. "How'd they get here?"

Later that evening over supper, Dad and Aidan recounted what they had seen on their walk. The back-and-forth of their shared adventure had knitted them together. But still I had to laugh; her confidence mixed with his love led them to an inaccurate conclusion. These rocks didn't come from space; they fell from the canyon rim. The next day, Dad napped, and I took a walk with Aidan. Again, the big rocks were on her mind.

"Mom, these rocks are so big they just had to come from space. I don't see any volcanoes, and they are just so big!" For fifteen minutes she continued her original hypothesis. When natural silence fell over us and our attention was given to wildflowers, I asked, "What else do you notice about the big rocks?" The simple question launched her into new, more accurate observations and conclusions. Later, we walked through the information center. She asked questions about the rim rocks to the park rangers; she looked at the pictures; she searched for the answers to her questions.

Aidan was at play. In this state of playful encounter and openness, uncertainty fueled her searching. Her curiosity stayed hot, as did her connection with Dad, me, and the canyon. Her searching was not fearful; it was without pressure or judgment, but rather was infused with the delight of discovery. This began our multi-year conversation about the rocks at the Black Canyon. The process of easy conversation around discovery brought us together. It was a delight to witness. Our time together wasn't focused on right information; it was about growing relationship and fueling wonder. I suspected that if she continued to engage with the rocks, she would arrive at the facts, but the facts weren't our only concern: connection was. Each trip invited her to a deeper understanding of and a deeper connection with the facts and the truth of the canyon.

Our conversations come back to my mind as we visit the canyon rim again many years later. Now, these wondering children are adults and know more of the facts associated. Aidan now knows that the rocks at the river came from the canyon rim, but what keeps her coming back, what shaped her relationship with the land and her family, was the time learning together. I wonder: what of our theological thinking might God permit, even while it is massively inaccurate, so that we can continue in conversation and wonder with our Divine Parent?

Could it be, as Paul says, that "we see through a glass, darkly"— but that the darkness might be part of the process of learning and wondering with God (1 Corinthians 13:12 KJV)? Accurate answers are important, but often they end the conversation. Once we arrive at the answer, we stop looking; we stop asking; we stop wondering.

The major distinction of childhood from adulthood is that children are naturally learners. We prefer the quick answers rather than the extended amount of time and energy that it takes to try, to fail, to try again. We chafe against the time it takes to learn. "When we're children, we're devoted to learning about our world and imagining all the other ways that world could be. When we become adults, we put all that we've learned and imagined to use."[4] But our learning and living isn't actually all that linear. Rather, we can lean into the circular nature of all things and continue to learn and change and grow throughout our lives.

CYCLE OF LEARNING

My friend and colleague Lynn Clouser Holt often says, "Perfection is the enemy of the good." The first time I heard her say that, it caught me off guard. How can that be, I wondered? Didn't Jesus say in the Sermon on the Mount, "Be perfect, therefore, as your heavenly Father is perfect" (Matthew 5:48)?

This saying deserves closer attention. It comes after the Beatitudes, where Jesus welcomes all those who have been thought to be excluded from God's kingdom. It comes after Jesus reminds his listeners of their identity as children of God who are salt and light. It comes after he reminds them what salt and light look like in the world: loving enemies, being faithful, forgiving, and free from contempt. Then, Jesus circles back to the centrality of our identity as children of God and caps it off with the charge for perfection . . . or so it seems.

R. C. Sproul writes that a better interpretation of the word *perfect* is the concept of being "whole" or "complete."[5] Each of the passages in Matthew 5 contains a relational disconnection, a breach, a break, a shattering. Religious fracture (the law and the prophets), relational fracture (anger, adultery, and divorce), and a fracture of faithfulness to the self (oaths and retaliation). Six times in this passage Jesus says some variation of "You have heard it said . . . but I say . . ." This is a classic setup for learning: Jesus takes what they already know and moves them one more step toward wholeness, one more step toward clearing the dark glass. Twice he roots their identity in being a child of God. And children are free to learn.

With a measure of reckless abandon and one or two nuggets of speculation, children take what they've got and offer it to the world. They are comfortable with correction, because for them, it is part of being a young person in an old world. Jesus is not inviting his listeners to puritan nitpicking; he is inviting them to return to their natural state as learners, young students in God's living classroom.

Turns out, my friend Lynn knows something about God's generous way, a way where even mistakes are included in the kingdom of God. This way is the way where sin and wounds are not throwaway items; they are fodder for transformation. Jesuit Anthony DeMello offers this little seedling: "Be grateful for your sins. They are carriers of grace."[6] And the Trappist monks at Saint Joseph's Abbey in Spenser, Massachusetts, drink and eat out of two-handed mugs that are reminiscent of cups that children learn to use.[7] It is a reminder to embrace the faith and humility of children.

This idea first became real to me one Sunday. For three weeks, my house had been full of guests. I was in sensory overload and really was all done with words, cooking, and cleaning. I have a longing to be hospitable, I really do. It has been written into my Rule of Life for more than two decades, but here's the thing—I'm kinda crappy at it.

I'm a creature of routine and having guests and extending hospitality disrupts that routine. When speaking about spiritual transformation, Dallas Willard writes about training "off the spot" for when we are "on the spot."[8] One would think that over twenty years of raising children would be enough off-the-spot training to form gracious hospitality within me, but still I struggle.

I needed fresh air and conversation that didn't use words. So, I skipped church and took a walk instead. Ridgway is a town not too far from where I live. The Uncompahgre River runs through it and into a state park about three miles north. I walked along the river for the better part of four hours before I felt I had walked out most of what ailed me. My legs and knees were aching, so I found a bench just next to the river and sat a while. It was a chilly winter afternoon, but the sun was shining, warming my face. The warmth felt like an invitation to really rest with my whole body. I stretched out on the bench, wanting to expose as much of my body to the sun as possible. Something like, "Look! Here I am. Do your healing work."

With my eyes closed, I began to feel the warmth spreading through my body. My thoughts slowed, as did my breathing. Even the winter wind even stilled. In the midst of that quiet moment, I could hear the water flowing over the cobblestone edges of the river. To my left, upstream, the water was flowing quickly, with force; every now and then, I could hear a knocking sound. I popped one eye open to make sure I was still alone, without a wildlife visitor who might want my spot.

All I saw was rushing water, flowing calmly, with intention over, under, and around the rocks. Content I was safely alone, I closed my eyes and listened once more. In my imagination, I could see the rocks with jagged edges uncovered by rushing water. With each season that passed, the water helped to shape those rocks, knocking off rounded edges. But those knocked-off bits weren't wasted. Indeed, nature knows nothing of waste. The knocked-off edges become part of the riverbed. In a small act of symbiosis, the water and the knocked-off pebbles help to stabilize the bed itself; together, they shape and form where this water will flow. The broken edges become nutrients to pinyon pine, rabbitbrush, and junegrass.

I thought of Jesus' words: "Let anyone who is thirsty come to me, and let the one who believes in me drink. As the scripture has said, 'Out of the believer's heart shall flow rivers of living water'" (John 7:37-38). Ah, yes; this river too is living, working all things for the eventual good of all. I wondered: what was being broken in me? What sharp edges were being removed and then used for my good and God's glory?

Paul tells us in 1 Corinthians 13:12, "For now we see in a mirror, dimly, but then we will see face to face. Now I know only in part; then I will know fully, even as I have been fully known." Paul's words suggest that our attempts at rational knowledge right now may be missing something. I am not saying that clear, sound reasoning lacks importance. But I wonder how the fear of not getting "it" right—or the impossible desire to "know fully" right now—may be holding us back from deeper intimacy with God.

Welcoming Practices

Find freedom. Reflect on the saying that "perfection is the enemy of the good." In what ways are you holding back because you are debilitated by the need to be perfect? Is there something that you are normally obsessive about that could use the cool wind of release and freedom?

Consider failure. Confession coming, prepare accordingly—I am an Enneagram 3. I would rather chew off my right arm than admit failure. Whenever I fail or come up short (or whatever you want to call it), I lock the experience away as quickly as I can, or I wallow in the failure. I drink every last drop of humiliation (perceived or real, doesn't matter) and let it redefine who I am. But neither of these ways of dealing with failure are good for body or soul. Remember the way the river wears down sharp rocks to nourish the soil? Understanding the redemptive power of God's kingdom is a game changer. What is your relationship with your failures? How could they lead to a deeper love of God, acceptance of self, and welcome of others?

Learn from a book. Read *I Am Enough* by Grace Byers and Keturah Bobo; start a conversation with the Spirit around the freedoms you might have if you lived as if you were enough. Or read *Wangari Maathai: The Woman Who Planted Millions of Trees* by Franck Prevot and Aurélia Fronty. Settle into this book as a learning experience. What do you notice about Wangari's life that speaks to you? Are there invitations from the Spirit for you woven throughout the story and its illustrations?

10

Pay Attention

The Truth you seek is not hidden from you; you simply do not notice it. It is here for you if you will only awake.

REB YERACHMIEL BEN YISRAEL

We call her NeeNee and she's got the best sense of humor around. She's the best playmate and grandmother I could have asked for. One day, she stayed with my kids while I went to lunch with a friend, and she channeled her goodness to her great-grandchildren. When I arrived home, fully satiated with good food and even better conversation, I found NeeNee lying on the couch with half a roll of toilet paper wrapped around her head. Six-year-old Aidan was standing near, plastic hacksaw in hand, immediately reassuring me, "Don't worry, Mama. Nee was sleeping so I took her brain out, but I'll put in back in later."

Since that day, NeeNee has often joked that maybe Aidan didn't actually put her brain back as God intended. Blessed are those who are fully awake, for they shall keep their brains and learn to be fully awake.

As a person who has been around children since I was one, I have said the phrase "pay attention" thousands of times. My faulty assumption has been that children are lost in some dream world, subjected to the whims of childish distraction, cut off from what is happening around them. Children have graciously expanded my understanding.

One autumn day long ago, I took my third-grade class on a field trip to a pumpkin farm and apple orchard on the outskirts of Rochester, New York. All thirty-one of us rode the city bus through the winding inner-city streets into the vibrant rural countryside. Not once did I need to invite the children to pay attention; they were paying attention to everything. As we got off the bus, they were paying attention to the mud underneath their feet. They were paying attention to the prickly feel of the pumpkin vines, the various shapes and sizes, and the smooth ridges that were begging to be touched. They were paying attention to the sweet smell of fried donuts and wet leaves. They were paying attention to the crunch of the Empire apple and the tart taste that caused their jaws to ache. The senses of these thirty-one children were tuned in; their attention was fully engaged with the world around them.

INNER AWAKENING

I sat across from Cassie and listened as she told of moving from place to place as a child. Her adaptability and resiliency meant that she could shift and change to fit into new surroundings in an instant. And while the skill had protected her and helped her to survive, it also masked her true self. She could no longer hear her own desires, her own likes, or her own wants. She could no longer get at the heart of her core self. She was at the point in her life where she longed to be who God had truly created her to be, but she had no idea who that was. The invitation to pay attention was in front of her. I asked her several questions about her longings, her desires, and what gave her life, but they were muddled over by decades of adaptability.

In what surely was a prompt by the Spirit, I remembered that each person was made in the image and likeness of God. So rather than circling the same spot repeatedly, I asked her to talk about the attributes of God that were most appealing to her. She said that she knew God was gracious. God had met her more than halfway and enabled her and strengthened her on many occasions. She said that God was patient with her as she struggled. She had experienced God's presence through years of suffering. God was steady, sure, and didn't leave at the first sign of trouble.

I then asked her if these attributes resonated in any way with who she was at the core of her being. Her eyes filled with tears; she could hardly speak. But I knew from firsthand witness that she embodied these attributes; we had been friends for ten years. In her faith community, she was well-known as gracious, meeting people more than halfway, enabling them and strengthening them on many occasions. She was patient with her children's struggles. She had been selflessly taking care of her dying mother throughout the past month, and, as a hospice nurse, her mother wasn't the only person she had journeyed with through suffering. She was a faithful friend to many. She was stable, steady, and safe.

When she did finally speak, she said it was hard to believe that she shared some of God's "genetic code." To say that God is her Father, and that somehow she had inherited God's attributes, was more than she could imagine. She wondered what it would look like to live more freely, more awakened into the divine goodness within.

All of us, at the very core of who we are, have a divine spark that reflects God's character in some way. For God, this "genetic code" is consistent, permeating every ounce of God's being. For us, human beings we learn along the way. We struggle to consistently live out of that place of shared goodness. Our cells go rogue, and we morph into a cancer that is compulsively bent on destruction. Truth be told, we also lack capacity. We earthlings are finite beings, just not able to embody that much divine good.

Begin today to write down the attributes of God that resonate with you. (If you need a list to get you moving, try the fruits of the Spirit in Galatians 5.) What of God's character have you experienced over the course of time? Be very specific; include all the details that you can recall. Bring your ongoing list into your conversations with God. Tell God of these attributes; let it move you to prayer. Over the course of our lives, the practice of divine adoration offers a freedom from selfish compulsion, and it can help us to pay attention to who we are at the deepest places.

LISTENING TO THE WHISPER WITHIN

To be clear this is not about looking in the mirror and thinking that we are God. This is about remembering the truest parts of ourselves and therefore finding freedom from our compulsion to self-attend. When children are thoroughly cared for, they are free to be awake and participatory in the world around them. They don't have to tend to themselves; they know that someone else is. As we are able to fully embrace ourselves as a dwelling place of the living God, we become freer to be awake to the needs of the world.

I have a story for you all—but be warned that I come from a long line of storytellers, and while the stories are true enough, the facts may not be, well . . . factual. With this in mind, listen to the following story from my Grandma June, who is well past her ninety-year marker. She loves to tell stories of her time as the first woman cowhand on the ranch they lived on in Oklahoma. Her daddy was a cowhand on the Chapman-Barnard Ranch and the father of ten children. All but three were girls, and she didn't want to do "women's work." She wanted to be outside with her beloved father working cattle. But women didn't do that kind of work in those days, so she tucked her mop of blond, almost white, hair up under her cowboy hat to disguise her gender and planted her spindly frame on her horse.

June and her brother Mundy (this name has been changed to protect the guilty) frequently rode the fences. Riding fences is a regular task of the cowhand; fences keep cattle in, and cattle are sold for money. In the wide-open prairie land of Oklahoma, it's an important but monotonous job. The story goes that June and Mundy were tasked with riding the fence on a blustery winter day. Wrapped in her coat made of waxed canvas, June left her hair down to insulate her against the cold wind. June and Mundy mounted their horses, glad to be free of indoor chores. The horses, thick with their winter coats, didn't particularly care about the cold. With warm human bodies on their backs and bellies full of hay, they were set for the day's work.

The first long stretch of fence was uneventful, easily ridden in an hour. The sun even decided to peek out and warm their faces. Scanning the fence line, Mundy could see that something about half of a mile ahead was hung up in the fence. His eyes must have caught sight about the same time that the horses caught sound or smell, because both stood stock-still and refused to move. The two found that no amount of kicking or swearing (the apple doesn't fall far from the tree) was going to move the horses. June and

Mundy climbed off their horses, tied them to the nearest cross post, and began walking toward whatever was hung in the fence. With every few steps their guesses ruled out particular possibilities. Too short to be a deer, too small to be a bear, too much fur to be a wild hog. The hair on the back of June's neck stood up. Her mind rifled through the other animal choices: coyote, badger, bobcat, and . . . oh, no. Mountain lion.

It is rare that mountain lions are seen, but June and Mundy saw in astonishment that one had found himself hung up in barbed wire. They saw that this wild cat was probably a young adolescent, and it was not doing well. Lethargic and hardly responding, whether due to cold or probably sickness, it barely lifted its head to face its human foes. Mundy, more confident (or stupid), walked right up to the defenseless animal. June, however, hung back by maybe fifty feet to give the animal space.

Both kids heard in their minds the voices of the adults in their lives: they should shoot the animal and drag it off the fence. If the animal were indeed dying, this would be an act of mercy. Then they could mend the fence and finish their job. But June heard another voice, her voice, a voice that had always echoed in her head and heart. It was a voice of relentless compassion and often out of place on the ranch. It asked her, "I wonder if we could save the poor animal?" Almost unconsciously, she asked the question aloud.

In the company of adults whose goal is efficiency and survival, her voice would have been ignored at best and shamed at worst. But she was not with adults; she was with her brother, whose compassion matched her own, and her question resonated with him. He agreed, and they hatched a plan.

They decided to put the animal in a sack and bring him home, where they hoped they could nurse him back to health. As fast as their cold legs could carry them, they ran back to their horses. June had a burlap sack shoved inside her saddlebag, which was carrying a bit of bread and long-gone-cold breakfast potatoes. Not ones to waste food, they quickly ate their lunch and ran to the mountain lion. They were hoping that their leather gloves and waxed-canvas coats would protect them if the lion suddenly turned on them.

Flanking the lion, they carefully slid the sack over the head and along the body. The sack was big enough to cover most of the cat, with only the creature's long tail hanging out. Mundy came from behind and picked up the cat, deadly ends facing outwards, but he didn't flinch at Mundy's touch. June ran back and gathered the horses. The two started making their way back home, the cat unnaturally still even while being jostled on the ride, and June, walking beside Mundy with reins in hand, silently tried on words to explain the situation with all the flair for the persuasive she had. She and Mundy worked out part two of their plan: they would put the cat in the cage they used to trap hogs. They would offer warm milk and keep it in the barn.

Back at home, their mom was watching for them. She came running when she saw they were walking, not riding, and that they were carrying something not so small. The word *surprise* doesn't completely convey her reaction when she saw the long tail hanging out of the burlap sack. June, ever the fast talker, dumped the whole story, hoping to overwhelm her mother's snap-decision skills by the sheer number of words. As one who revels in surprises of her own, Mother sent June to put up the horses in the barn and bring the hog cage to the kitchen. "The kitchen?" both children whispered—but they obeyed.

The wild cat was in fact alive, just barely. It took June and Mother only about three days to nurse it back to health. On the fourth day, the young mountain lion was well enough to terrorize every person who walked through the kitchen. The new problem was how to set the animal free while staying just outside the reach of its sharp claws. Eventually, they used two broomsticks to push the cage so that its door was flush against the open kitchen door; with an old piece of pipe, they fiddled with the latch just long enough to spring it open. Then they ran like mad. The cat followed for just a few strides, but soon broke away toward the wild open prairie.

Reflecting on this story, June was attentive to what was stirring within her. Compassion and fear mingled in her mind and heart. Healthy fear can bring about respect and awe and lead to wisdom. Even a sick mountain lion demanded that. Unhealthy fear can give rise to phrenic reactions that shut out awareness. June's fear was of the healthy variety, which made it possible for her to hear the Spirit's voice that whispered compassion for a wounded creature. Children are often more awake to tenderness and compassion than their adult counterparts. I wonder: when compassion and fear mingle in your heart, what would it look like to awaken to tenderness?

CENTURIES OF PRACTICE

For centuries, the people of God have been practicing being awake. We catch a glimpse of this practice in the life of Daniel. You might remember Daniel and the lion's den from childhood Bible stories. Daniel was a captive in Babylon and came into a position of power. He was so successful that the king's underlings wanted to get rid of him. They saw that the only ground for complaint against him was "in connection with the law of God," so they conspired to have the king sign an edict condemning to a den of lions whoever prayed to another that was not the king.

Daniel was in a land that didn't follow the God he freely knew in his childhood. His God had accompanied him in good and bad, through betrayal and trauma, through promotion and prison. Now, Daniel wanted to keep company with God no matter where life took him, no matter what situations and global catastrophes were present. In verse ten of Daniel chapter six, we get one tiny glimpse of how he did that.

> Although Daniel knew the document had been signed he continued to go to his house, which had windows in its upper room open toward Jerusalem, and to get down on his knees three times a day to pray to his God and praise him, just as he had done previously. (Daniel 6:10)

Three times a day, Daniel turned his whole self, body included toward God. Three times a day, he reminded himself to wake up. Surrounded by a hostile community, with feelings of warranted fear, Daniel paused and let God remind him of the reality of things.

Children carry Daniel's wisdom with them. When my kids were little, going to the park was a treat. Once a week, I met with a group of women for prayer and study; those of us who were home-schooling schlepped our children along too. The kids met new people and played quite happily without adult intervention. This park was suitably equipped with a steep metal slide that brought just the right amount of danger. Either you fell from the unrailed landing after summiting ten feet of narrow steps, or you blistered your bare legs on the red-hot griddle of a slide made fiery by the high-altitude sun. If that wasn't enough peril, a few spins on the merry-go-round helped you retaste your lunch. The monkey bars weren't menacing until another kid decided to challenge your ability to hang on for dear life. Not one child lost an eye, but bruised bodies and rumpled feelings sometimes occurred. Still, this was adventurous living for young children.

One afternoon, while we adults gathered discussing the merits of parenting as mild persecution (a testing of our faith that might cost us everything), I noticed something. While the children were on the playground, they would occasionally stop and look for their parents. While playing, my kids would raise their heads and move to a place where they could see me and be seen. If they couldn't catch my eye and connect with a glance, they would stop whatever they were doing and come to me. Not really to ask for anything, but to be present—not more than a moment—for a touch, a hug, a hello for connection. Then they were back to playing, the good work of being a child.

Much later, I learned that this behavior was what secure attachment looked like. When we are securely attached, we have freedom to go and do what is ours to do. We can be who we are with freedom and light. We can explore and test. The glance back, the pause, or the touchstone is to remind us of who we are; it is to remind us of the reality of being a beloved one safe in the arms of one who loves us.

Children practice this pause and we adults do it too, especially with God. We are born with beginning attachments to God. Our expectations of safety and care are alive and well. As we grow up, we need an ongoing connection with God, even as we do the work that we are called to do, whether we are parents or plumbers or both. Adults can forget our ongoing need to stay awake to God's presence; we can start to buy into the illusion that we are in this alone, that the wounds and wanderings of our living go unseen and without care. This way of living is not really living. It is painful, and we will do whatever we can to get some relief from the pain. We nurture false attachments that can never take the place of a true attachment to God, our Divine Parent. These false attachments are objects that may be in themselves good gifts given to us for enjoyment. But we become dependent on them asking them to do to what they cannot.

We look to people, positions, possessions, and potions of all kinds. These cannot give us what we most deeply desire, but they can lull us to sleep. They can, for a short period of time, move us into a state of not feeling our pain. We can be lulled to a kind of zombie sleep by the demands surrounding us. Work, family, church, responsibilities, even good social justice work—these can be tasks we do, not because they flow out of our living and loving with God, but because we are running from our pain. In essence, these false attachments trick us into thinking that we are awake to reality when we are actually asleep.

Daniel's three-times-a-day glance back at God kept him awake and connected. Three times a day he stopped and, like an adult child connecting to his God, his Divine Parent, he touched their shared connection. He drank in divine love and reality. And we all know what happens next. Daniel went through a terrible trial where his very life was in danger. While being hurled into a lion's den may not be a common occurrence for human beings, still, living is inherently dangerous. Our finite human bodies get sick and die. Trauma and tragedy are all around us. We must, if we are to stay awake, keep our finger on the reality that we have a Divine Parent who is with us through it all.

The first mention of the name Immanuel is in Isaiah 7:14, where it represents a signpost for a present and future hope that indeed,

God was and is with the people. To be sure that we understand, Matthew quotes Isaiah and then opens it up a bit more directly: "'And they shall name him Emmanuel,' which means, 'God is with us'" (Matthew 1:23). I suppose God could have named himself "God fixes us," or "God judges us." Or "God mocks us." Or even "God puts up with us."

Instead, God acts out of love and compassion and breaches heaven and earth and (if you ask our Eastern Orthodox sisters and brothers) kicks in the gates of hell to be with us. This is what love looks like. God chose to be Emmanuel. God is with us from a place of love. God is not repelled by human beings but drawn to us: love looks like that. Being with God is the most awake a human being can be. A life awake is one filled with love and holy foolishness. It can be risky, and freakishly dangerous. Our Mothering Father is as near as our very breath if we are only awake.

THE PRACTICE OF WAKING UP

A common term we use today that describes the trend of awakening to injustice in the world is "woke." While there's a lot of good coming from these movements, such trends can move us back into a state of sleeping as we mark ourselves "right" on a particular issue. Once we tick the box, we (if we do not suffer with the injustice daily) can go back to sleep.

Instead, we need to practice staying awake, keeping our thinking and praying and connecting active and alive. Christian tradition has a name for this practice of staying awake and in touch with God: fixed-hour prayer. Fixed-hour prayer essentially is turning toward God at certain times throughout the day; it is basically praying-without-ceasing using a system. The systematizing of the prayer makes it easier to pray together in a community, even a dispersed one. Praying at certain times of the day didn't end in the Hebrew Scriptures with Daniel but continued with the Jewish people into the stories in the New Testament. We catch a glimpse of the practice in Acts 3, 10, and 16. The people of the Way gathered and collectively turned toward God, made contact, and stayed awake.

I first started to practice fixed-hour prayer out of desperation. For reasons still unknown to me, Anwen didn't sleep for the first nine months of her life. Perhaps she was just too full of life and light in her new surroundings. Perhaps she wanted to be sure she had the upper hand for the next eighteen years—who knows? But I do know that if babies don't sleep, parents don't sleep. This kid had (and still has) pipes to match her energy level. She wasn't just awake; she was loud about it. One night, while trying to convince my little party animal that she needed to sleep so that mama had a fighting chance at sanity the next day, I decided to pray a nighttime liturgy called the Night Office. Perhaps it was sleep deprivation, perhaps it was hormonal, or perhaps it was postpartum depression, but I couldn't stop crying. I felt alone and like a total failure in my mothering both to this brand-new wonder and to Aidan, who was only three years old and simply wanted her mama to be as present as she used to be.

I can't remember how I got it or how a Baptist-raised kid knew about fixed-hour prayer, but I used a little book by Phyllis Tickle called *Divine Hours: Pocket Edition*. My copy still smells like soured breast milk and is delightfully "illustrated" by said three-year-old.

I began with the Night Office because I was awake and lonely and needed to know that there were others who were up and praying the same words. Each night I prayed, "O God, come to my assistance; O Lord, make haste to help me."[1] Each night, Sunday through Saturday, I prayed a snippet of Psalms, an invitation to bring the reality of the life I was living to this God who was with me in the struggle. In the short readings, I learned just a bit about my sisters and brothers in our big family of God. Somehow (by the tricky grace of the Spirit) I realized that even as God was with me, so were all those who had already gone before. Saint Francis, Thomas à Kempis, Catherine of Siena, Chrysostom, and so many others. These adult children of God, who are part of the great cloud of witnesses, were with God and with me.

In her book *Seven Sacred Pauses: Living Mindfully Through the Hours of the Day,* Macrina Wiederkehr says that "living mindfully is the art of living awake and ready to embrace the gift of the present moment."[2] *Seven Sacred Pauses* walks the reader through the seven fixed hours of prayer as an opportunity to pause, to awaken, and connect with what is most real. We don't pray these hours out of guilt; we pray them because we long to be grounded and rooted in connective love. Through my little practice, I found fellowship in the night. The dark reality of my sleeping situation and mental health wasn't removed; rather, I found that in the darkness there was a mysterious community that welcomed me just as I was.

AWAKEN YOUR BRAIN AND BODY

Young children live in a perpetual state of awareness, but adult habits and patterns have functionally put us to sleep. These habitual patterns of living make it possible for our limited consciousness to focus on what we have prioritized as most important—or most distracting—at the moment. But they also put us to sleep to the new or subtle ways the Spirit might be at work in the world. We can counter the snooze-inducing effects with a simple practice.

Travel. Take your body to a place, a community, that you have never experienced. While I'm writing this during the fifty-second surge of Covid-19, travel feels like a pipe dream. But I've started packing my suitcase and just dragging it around the living room. Even if you stay in your own town, try a new park, a new grocery store. Join a gym or club outside of your typical community.

Our driving need to find safety in sameness is killing not only our minds but our world. God, it seems, is quite fond of diversity. Just look around a bit. Living things are so completely diverse. Even when twins share the same DNA, their experiences shape them to be different. Difference is the trajectory of the creative good. We can try to make cookie-cutter homes, people, lawns, and laws, but diversity just won't have it. Even cookie-cutter cookies won't have it! In the baking, each cookie develops differently.

However, taking our bodies to places of difference is not enough. We must go into new and different experiences with our wonderment on full tilt. The younger a child is, the more robust their wonderment. The way a child and an adult encounter a new experience is generally quite different. Adults have learned caution, the analysis of risk and reward. And to be certain, these are skills that keep us alive and functioning in the world. However, these skills have a shadow side in that they put the kibosh on wonderment. A child who is fluent in wonderment will be compelled to engage with all the dimensions of their self; they will need to taste, touch, see, hear, and smell. We adults can recover our wonderment by pushing the edges of old patterns and habits. After you have arrived at this place of difference, risk a little and experience what might be new to you.

Become curious about why and how things are done. Listen and learn; welcome and try that which is before you. Name goodness, beauty, and truth where you find it, for these are evidence of God's presence.

Welcoming Practices

Notice your longings. First, begin to notice your own longings. As adults we have often had to shut our ears to our inner desires. Twice a day check in with your desires. In the morning: perhaps before you get out of bed, reflect on this question, What do I want for this day? And in the evening: perhaps just before you fall asleep: What do I want for my sleep tonight? Formulate this desire into a prayerful request.

Listen deeply to desire. Surface desire is different from deep desire. Surface desire is often fueled by reaction. Deep desire is fueled by our deepest and truest self in concert with the Divine. When paying attention to your desire this week, ask yourself, "What is fueling this desire?"

Learn from a book. Read *Wonder Walkers* by Micha Archer. What wonderings come to mind as you engage with this book? If you are up for a longer read, try Rachel Carson's *The Sense of Wonder.*

Conclusion

Born a Mystic

Mysticism is the passionate longing of the soul for God.

EVELYN UNDERHILL

Every one of us has been born a mystic. We are made to experience God. Our first and most natural inclination is to connect with God in deeply bonding, yet often very ordinary ways.

I have learned this from the children at Haven House. Joseph and his family had been at Haven House for two months, and I had met with him a handful of times in Holy Listening. Holy Listening is one-on-one spiritual accompaniment for children. Joseph's brown hair was matted on one side of his head. Clearly, he had just woken up and hadn't seen a bath in a while. "Hi, Joseph, glad to see you!" I called out as I entered the doors of Haven House.

"Tia Lacy," he said. "Can I come to Holy Listening today?"

"Yeah, mijo; let me get the room set up."

Joseph joined me on the white blanket that marks our sacred listening space. "You know how those kids at school keep talking smack to me and blaming me?" I nodded my head, as this was a common story for Joseph.

"Well yesterday I was doin' like, nothing, and they were all, you know. But then I went to the swings, there was only one left. And I started to swing and do that breathing thing, 'God is with me, I am safe.' And it was like God swirled all around me and I forgot those kids and . . ."

He fell silent and still, looking up in the corner of the room, like he was remembering something that he couldn't find words for. Then he shrugged his shoulders and shook his head. "It was like God . . . oh, I don't know. I stayed on the swings until my teacher made me come in."

Evelyn Underhill names the central fact of the mystic's experience as "an overwhelming consciousness of God and of his own soul: a consciousness which absorbs or eclipses all other centres of interest."[1] On the swings that day, Joseph had an experience of God and of himself that sidelined all his other concerns. The experience made such a mark on him that he wanted to stay with it and wanted to tell someone who might believe him. We could say that Joseph had a mystical experience of God.

Of all the difficult things to explain to children, we might think that unitive consciousness might win the complexity medal, but we'd be wrong. Children live in the dance between self-discovery, healthy separation, and deep attachments to their caregivers. Depending on where they are in the dance, unity is never far away. It brings to mind the well-known study of a very young child sitting with their mother looking into a mirror.[2] When a dollop of whipped cream is placed on their mother's face, they try to wipe it off their own face, not quite realizing that the one of them are two. Unity they know; separation they learn. It seems that *conscious* knowledge of God is required after the development of reason, but experiences of God, divine unity, happens long before consciousness. Mystical experiences are both beyond reason and before it.

To begin in unconscious union is not to say that there isn't work to do. Attention and intention, walking the spiral into conscious union, is an invitation from God. The work and the journey, however, do not negate the truth that union with God, conscious or not, is our true home. This union with God is the place from which love flows in and through us.

Settle into these words of Jesus' childlike wisdom:

> At that time Jesus said, "I thank you, Father, Lord of heaven and earth, because you have hidden these things from the wise and the intelligent and have revealed them to infants; yes, Father, for such was your gracious will. . . . Come to me, all you that are weary and are carrying heavy burdens, and I will give you rest. Take my yoke upon you, and learn from me; for I am gentle and humble in heart, and you will find rest for your souls. For my yoke is easy, and my burden is light." (Matthew 11:25-26, 28-30)

In the last ten chapters, we have explored what our Mothering Father has revealed to children. We have wandered bravely through wonder and wounds and found that God is with us. We have pondered humility, attachment, play, imagination, humor, and presence. We have welcomed our bodies and welcomed the freedom to learn. Irish poet John O'Donohue, who seemed to be quite childlike himself, understood this circular human pilgrimage we take from being a beloved infant in God's tender care to being God's adult children. He writes:

> It would be lovely in old age, as the body sheds its power, if each of us who would be pilgrims into that time could shed

the false gravity and the weight that we carry for a lot of our lives and if we could enter our old age almost like a baby enters childhood, with the same kind of gracefulness, of possibility, and the same kind of innocence, but a second innocence rather than a first one.[3]

But we can't simply read about this process; we must experience it with our whole selves. This I learned with two friends, Roxy and Tucker, who I met through the Renovaré Institute for Spiritual Formation. It was Tucker's spiritual practice since his sister died to randomly jump into bodies of water: a river, pond, inlet, or ocean. The simple, sacred, and sometimes sloppy act made space for his grief and was a reminder that he, himself, was living. He shared this practice with me and others during a week-long retreat in Washington state. He was going to jump into Puget Sound at some point, and did I want to go?

Did I want to take my body, with all it held, squeeze it into a swimsuit, and jump into the ice-cold ocean? Yes, of course I did.

There were two of us, Roxy and me, who were childlike enough to go with Tucker to the sound on this partially cloudy day. Roxy is a dear friend, honest, funny, and lives just this side of holy foolery. Tucker had come prepared with a small (what I mean is *tiny*) blow-up raftish kind of thing made for two people and rigged with a trolling motor. Roxy and I sat on the pier while he loaded this LEGO life raft into the sound; we talked about what it meant to be women with bodies, and the challenges of welcoming and accepting those bodies. He drove the little boat up the pier, and we gingerly entered the craft. The trolling motor didn't stand a chance, but it tried really hard to buzz us around the sound until we found a spot that was just right for jumping. While the practice itself held sorrow, our tone wasn't somber but filled with a holy laughter. People on the shore were staring and, no doubt, joining in our laughter.

Once we found a spot, he stopped the motor and we fell silent. What did it mean to be fully alive and breathing in the goodness of the Eternal One who longed us into being? It meant gathering with dear friends in a tiny Barbie boat and then jumping into an ocean of God's love. It was cold, no doubt. And as soon as we hit the water, we all laughed, remembering that indeed, we were living. I had no idea what else was with us in the murky depths (and thank God for rabid ignorance), but I didn't care. I also had no idea how I was going to get back into the boat (think beached manatee, very maternal and quite gelatinous), but, again, that didn't matter. Together, we celebrated life in God in the one way that was most true, most natural, most real—as children.

Roxy, who is master wordsmith and a truly good listener, wrote the following poem. Read it through a time or three, listen for Eternal Child calling your name.

ETERNAL CHILD

Roxy Humphrey

"Jerusalem will be called the Faithful City. . . . And the
    streets of the city shall be full of [children] playing in its
    streets." (Zechariah 8:3, 5)

Eternal Child,

You who know that when we are most faithful to You—
    to ourselves—
we are also most like children:
freely playing in the streets
and negotiating justice
and equality

and fair game
in each present moment.
Some of us have never known
what it is like to know carefree,
wild, and joyous play.
And many of us have forgotten.
Grow from within that vulnerable, honest,
innocence that we see in the small ones around us.
May it grow to the point that we can shed ourselves
of our adult skin and be what we most truly are:
children.
Amen.[4]

Welcoming Practices

Reflect. My friend and teacher Trevor Hudson often says that we don't learn from our experiences (bold, but a true statement if I've ever heard one). Instead, we learn from our reflecting on experiences. So, I'd like to invite you to wander back through the time we've spent together. Reflect on the ideas, words, images, and practices that resonated with you. Savor the good ways the Spirit met you in these pages and practices. Then reflect on your resistance. What parts twisted your knickers? What was that about? Invite the Spirit to help you understand what your faithfulness requires.

Gather a group. Do you know a friend or two who might be helped by this book and the practices? Gather together and feel free to make use of the discussion guide. Savor a bit of conversation with one another around the content.

Acknowledgments

To these who have showed me how to welcome my childlike self with freedom and raucous delight. Jean and Dave Nevills, Lynn Clouser Holt, Gary and Regina Moon, Trevor Hudson, Chris Hall, and Ross Tatum, I am forever grateful.

Questions for Reflection and Discussion

Each session is framed by two themes: Scripture and story. Take a generous swath of time to engage with the Scripture passage together. Read it aloud slowly. Perhaps read it a few times. Then use the questions to share what you notice in your own self, what you notice in the passage. Notice where the Spirit is drawing your attention. Notice what memories or moments from your own life might be given light through Scripture.

Then move to the story portion. Stories are where we live out the realities of our lives. Story is where the rubber meets the road, where we hold our living and loving in the light of Christ. In this portion, there are invitations to reflect on both the stories within the chapter and your own story. We need brave spaces to tell the stories of our wounds and allow others to bear witness with open hearts. The members of the group are to be witnesses, not fixers of wounds. Listen with your full presence and praying heart—but leave the fixing to God.

Some of the questions are quite vulnerable. Can I encourage you to guard your vulnerability? There are times when we sense it is time to tap our brave selves and share the tender details of our lives. And there are also times when the bravest thing we can do is say, "I'll pass on this one." Both are most certainly welcome. Never underestimate the value of your listening presence.

SESSION ONE: INTRODUCTION, CHAPTERS 1 AND 2

Scripture: Matthew 18:1-5.

What is your initial response to this passage?

What childhood memories or moments come to the surface?

How do you feel about those memories or moments?

What do you notice about Jesus?

How might Jesus speak to you about your memory?

How is your journey like Eve's or Adam's? (It might not be gender specific.)

Story:

How would you answer the question, What is God like?

How have you experienced the masculine dimension of God?

How have you experienced the feminine dimension of God?

What metaphor describes your relationship with God? (Perhaps: committed partners, parent/child, business associates . . .)

What do you sense Jesus is saying to you concerning your childhood self?

How has life been like a spiral or Celtic knot for you?

SESSION TWO: CHAPTERS 3 AND 4

Scripture: 1 Corinthians 13, Psalm 23.

What aspect of God speaks to you from 1 Corinthians 13?

What aspect do you hope (but may not know for sure) is true?

What do you think might be the difference between childlike and childish?

What do you think the connection is between faith (trust), hope, and love?

How has God been a good shepherd to you?

Take a moment and reflect on my paraphrase of Psalm 23. What resonates or doesn't resonate with you?

Story:

What did you notice about your picture of God in relation to these Scripture readings?

What do you recognize you know "only in part"?

How have people loved you well?

Share a story of wonder, mystery, awe, tears, nature, woven threads of meaning, or unity.

If this group seems safe to you, tell the story of one of your bodily wounds. It could be a scar on your forehead you got while playing Spiderman with your brother, or it could be something much more tender.

What is one thing you can do this week to welcome or honor your body?

SESSION THREE: CHAPTERS 5 AND 6

Scripture: Matthew 14:22-33, Ezekiel 47:1-12.

What do you notice about Jesus' playful posture?

Imagine yourself in the Matthew 14 story. Who are you? What are you doing?

Are there other stories from Jesus' life that seem playful to you?

Since bodies matter, what do you notice about the bodies in these passages?

Imagine the scene in Ezekiel 47. Which of your senses are ignited?

How might the water in the Ezekiel reading be like God's love and God's presence in the world? What else might it represent?

Story:

Share a story of how you play.

When do you lose track of time?

How do you feel about the idea of Jesus as playful?

What absurdities do you see in daily life?

What does a wide faith experience look like for you?

What does a deep faith experience look like for you?

SESSION FOUR: CHAPTERS 7 AND 8

Scripture: John 6:1-13.

What do you notice about the intersection between imagination, hope, and miracle?

Who are you in this story, and how does it speak to a particular circumstance in your life?

How does Jesus use his imagination at the service of love and connection?

Jesus asks the question "Where are we to buy bread?" to include others in what he was about to do. What including question is Jesus asking you?

What leftovers of God's generosity are you gathering these days?

What do you think the boy's response might have been to seeing Jesus use his lunch?

Story:

What has been your relationship with imagination? Include the positive and the negative.

How do you cocreate with God?

How does play and imagination infuse your work life?

What acts of holy foolery might be emerging for you?

How has laughter been a gift in hard times?

When have you witnessed true humility?

SESSION FIVE: CHAPTERS 9, 10, AND CONCLUSION

Scripture: Matthew 5.

What do you notice in the Beatitudes (Matthew 5:1-12)?

How might each Beatitude be a statement of God's inclusivity?

What salt or light do you see in others or the world around you?

In Matthew 5:21, Jesus begins his "you have heard" refrain. What does this refrain say to you about being a learner in God's big world?

What questions are stirring that need more conversation with Jesus?

What are you wondering about?

Story:

What failures, mistakes, or regrets come to mind?

When you bring these failures into conversation with God, what did you hear?

What have been the unexpected gifts of grace that have stayed with you?

What is giving you life right now?

In this second birth of childhood, what is God inviting you to?

How (get practical here) will you really, deeply live?

Notes

INTRODUCTION: WELCOMING THE CHILD WITHIN

[1]For more information, see my YouTube video: "What is Spiritual Direction," Lacy Borgo, www.youtube.com/watch?v=k7kJivgFwbM. You can find a spiritual director through SDIcompanions.org.

1. KNOWING GOD, ACCEPTING SELF

[1]Gerard W. Hughes, *Cry of Wonder* (London: Bloomsbury, 2014), 53.

[2]Wilda C. Gafney, *Womanish Midrash: A Reintroduction to the Women of the Torah and the Throne* (Louisville, KY: Westminster John Knox, 2017), 20. See also Mike Morrell, "'Biblical Proofs' for the Feminine Face of God in Scripture," *Mike Morrell* (blog), May 30, 2012, https://mikemorrell.org/2012/05/biblical-proofs-for-the -feminine-face-of-god-in-scripture/.

[3]Trevor Hudson, *Discovering Our Spiritual Identity: Practices for God's Beloved* (Downers Grove, IL: InterVarsity Press, 2010), 16.

[4]I unpack the push and pull of this power dynamic in my previous book *Spiritual Conversations with Children: Listening to God Together* (Downers Grove, IL: Inter-Varsity Press, 2020).

[5]Maggie Ross, *Writing the Icon of the Heart: In Silence Beholding* (Eugene, OR: Cascade Books, 2013), 3.

[6]When we consider family systems theory, we see that children will carry the un-peaceableness of their family. Their attachment to parents (either or both) means that they cannot separate themselves and therefore will pursue peace (not shalom) by taking on the anxiety and pain the parent possesses. To be clear, this is not a healthy state for the child (or anyone else), but it is a core need.

[7]Jerome Berryman, *Becoming Like a Child: The Curiosity of Maturity beyond the Norm* (New York: Church Publishing, 2017), 167.

[8]Karl Rahner, "Ideas for a Theology of Childhood," *Theological Investigations* (London: Cox & Wyman, 1982), 3:33-50.

2. REMEMBERING WONDER, REDEEMING WOUNDS

[1]You can read about this history in my doctoral dissertation: Lacy Finn Borgo, "Spiritual Direction with Children the Next Natural Step in the Christian Historical Progression of Children's Spiritual Formation" (DMin diss., George Fox University, 2016), https://digitalcommons.georgefox.edu/dmin/207/.

[2]Dallas Willard, "The Nature of Agape Love," Renovaré, https://renovare.org/articles /the-nature-of-agape-love.

[3]Maggie Ross, *Writing the Icon of the Heart: In Silence Beholding* (Eugene, OR: Cascade Books, 2013), 46.

3. REATTACHING TO OUR DIVINE PARENT

[1]Shelley E. Taylor, "Tend and Befriend Theory," in *Handbook of Theories of Social Psychology*, ed. Paul A. M. Van Lange, Arie W. Kruglanski, and E. Tory Higgins (London: Sage Publications, 2012), 1:32-49.

[2]For more information on Dr. Neufeld's excellent work, see the Neufeld Institute. He teaches on these stages in the *Family 360 Podcast*, www.family360podcast .com/ep-45-dr-gordon-neufeld-true-play-the-six-stages-of-attachment.

[3]Trevor Hudson and Jerry Haas outline this process in their teaching series and book, *The Cycle of Grace: Living in Sacred Balance* (Nashville, TN: Upper Room, 2012).

[4]Jonathan Sacks, *Not in God's Name: Confronting Religious Violence* (New York: Schocken Books, 2015), 172.

[5]Robert Coles, *The Spiritual Life of Children* (Boston: Houghton Mifflin, 1990); Rebecca Nye, *Children's Spirituality: What It Is and Why It Matters* (London: Church House, 2009); David Hay with Rebecca Nye, *The Spirit of the Child: Revised Edition* (London: Jessica Kingsley, 2006).

[6]Sacks, *Not in God's Name*, 172.

[7]Edward Robinson, *The Original Vision* (Oxford: Religious Experience Research, 1977).

[8]Dallas Willard, "Biblical and Theological Foundations for Spiritual Formation in Christ 2," October 11, 2011, https://conversatio.org/biblical-and-theological -foundations-for-spiritual-formation-in-christ-2/.

[9]Richard Rohr, "A Special Note from Fr. Richard: My Hope for This Community," *Apocalyptic Hope*, Center for Action and Contemplation, April 27, 2021, https://cac .org/daily-meditations/a-special-note-from-fr-richard-my-hope-for-this -community-2021-04-27/.

[10]Howard Thurman, *Jesus and the Disinherited* (Boston: Beacon Press, 1976), 19. This book should be read and reread by every Christ-follower. Thurman's astute understanding of the way of Christ for all people is a wisdom we need.

[11]This is a paraphrase of several translations.

4. ALL GOD'S CHILDREN GOT BODIES

[1] *Merriam-Webster*, s.v. "incarnate (v.)," accessed September 3, 2022, www.merriam-webster.com/dictionary/incarnate.

[2] Dallas Willard, *Renovation of the Heart: Putting on the Character of Christ* (Colorado Springs, CO: NavPress, 2002), 165.

[3] Dallas Willard, *Divine Conspiracy: Rediscovering Our Hidden Life in God* (New York: HarperCollins, 2009), chap. 2.

[4] To learn more, see "Desmond Tutu, Ubuntu and the Possibility of Hope," Looking for Wisdom, January 13, 2022, www.lookingforwisdom.com/ubuntu/.

[5] Randy Woodley's work is a good place to start learning about Indigenous theology and our connection to place: see www.randywoodley.com/new-books.

[6] Christine Valters Paintner, *Wisdom of the Body: A Contemplative Journey to Wholeness for Women* (Notre Dame, IN: Sorin Books, 2017), 2.

[7] "Jewish Women and BRCA Gene Mutations," *Bring Your Brave* Campaign, Center for Disease Control, September 27, 2021, www.cdc.gov/cancer/breast/young_women/bringyourbrave/hereditary_breast_cancer/jewish_women_brca.htm.

[8] Anne Lamott says that we get to tell our stories and that if people wanted us to write well of them, they should have behaved better (see her TED talk, "12 Truths I Learned from Life and Writing," at www.ted.com/talks/anne_lamott_12_truths_i_learned_from_life_and_writing?language=en). You might notice that I have not included the names of the boys who hurt me. Rest assured that they are real, and I remember them. However, you will have heard their praises sung in books, movies, and all other manner of cultural trash that promotes power and privilege above honor and connection. You may have experienced your own version of this pain. So, for you, I leave it blank. You may use the names you know.

[9] John O'Donohue, *Walking in Wonder: Eternal Wisdom for a Modern World* (New York: Convergent Books, 2015), 131.

[10] "Cast All Your Votes for Dancing," in *I Heard God Laughing: Poems of Hope and Joy: Renderings of Hafiz*, Daniel Ladinsky (New York: Penguin Books, 2006), 8; used with permission of Daniel Ladinsky. This poem is a "rendering" inspired by Hafiz.

5. THE SPIRITUALITY OF PLAY

[1] Thank you, Anwen, for graciously giving me permission to tell our shared story here.

[2] *The Inclusive Psalms* (Hyattsville, MD: Priests for Equality, 1997), 140.

[3] "Dr. Gordon Neufeld – The Essential Nature of Play," February 1, 2021, *Family 360 Podcast*, www.family360podcast.com/dr-gordon-neufeld-the-essential-nature-of-play/.

[4] "He Helped Us with Our Feelings," Fred Rogers Company, 2018, www.misterrogers.org/articles/he-helped-us-with-our-feelings/.

⁵Wright Thompson, "The Power Game," ESPN, www.espn.com/espn/eticket /story?page=090618/dchoops.

⁶Di Gammage, *Playful Awakening: Releasing the Gift of Play in Your Life* (London: Jessica Kingsley, 2017), 36.

⁷Personal correspondence with Dave Nevills, printed with permission.

⁸Stuart Brown, *Play: How It Shapes the Brain, Opens the Imagination and Invigorates the Soul* (New York: Penguin, 2010), 42.

⁹Brown, *Play*, 10-11.

¹⁰Gammage, *Playful Awakening*, 26.

¹¹James Martin, SJ, "The Most Infallible Sign," *America Magazine*, April 2, 2007, www .americamagazine.org/faith/2007/04/02/most-infallible-sign.

¹²In my opinion, poetry is best listened to. You can hear this poem read by Joanna Macy in the *On Being* podcast, September 16, 2010: https://onbeing.org/poetry /go-to-the-limits-of-your-longing/.

¹³Rainer Maria Rilke, "Go to the Limits of Your Longing," in *Rilke's Book of Hours: Love Poems to God*, trans. Anita Barrow and Joanna Macy (New York: Riverhead, 2005).

6. FOUNTAIN FLOWING DEEP AND WIDE

¹Jesse Joyner, "Who Wrote the Deep and Wide Song?" *Jesse Joyner Juggling* (blog), February 20, 2019, http://jessejoyner.com/who-wrote-the-deep-and-wide-song/.

²Alison Gopnik, *Philosophical Baby: What Children's Minds Tell Us About Truth, Love and the Meaning of Life* (New York: Farrar, Straus and Giroux, 2009), 110.

³Dallas Willard, *The Divine Conspiracy: Rediscovering Our Hidden Life in God* (San Francisco: Harper Collins, 1998), 62.

⁴C. S. Lewis, *Letters to Malcolm: Chiefly on Prayer* (San Diego: Harvest, 1964), 92-93.

⁵John O'Donohue, *Walking in Wonder: Eternal Wisdom for a Modern World* (New York: Convergent Books, 2015), 20.

⁶Thomas R. Kelly, *A Testament of Devotion* (New York: HarperCollins, 1941), 43.

7. IMAGINATE

¹Dallas Willard, *The Divine Conspiracy: Rediscovering Our Hidden Life in God* (San Francisco: Harper Collins, 1998), 80.

²Jesse White, *God's Invitation to Creative Play* (Wallingford, PA: Pendle Hill, 2021), 15-23.

³You can find this webinar with Makoto Fujimura, Margaret Campbell, and Carolyn Arends at Renovaré's website: https://renovare.org/events/art-faith.

⁴John O'Donohue, *Walking in Wonder: Eternal Wisdom for a Modern World* (New York: Convergent Books, 2015), 6.

[5]The Rule of St. Benedict as shared by the Abigail Adams Institute: https://static1 .squarespace.com/static/53b59f96e4b089bf6ae90076/t/5e2f635de7a3a371580 91976/1580163933393/TGC+Benedict.pdf.

8. HUMOR AND THE HOLY FOOL

[1]James Martin, SJ, *Between Heaven and Mirth: Why Joy, Humor, and Laughter Are at the Heart of the Spiritual Life* (New York: Harper One, 2011), 15.

[2]In his book *Between Heaven and Mirth*, Father James Martin explains that he searched high and low for written evidence of this quote but could find none. He was told that just because it wasn't written down, doesn't mean she didn't say it. Martin, *Between Heaven and Mirth*, 69.

[3]Howard Macy, *Laughing Pilgrims: Humor and the Spiritual Journey* (Waynesboro, GA: Paternoster Press, 2006), preface.

[4]Asta Cekaite and Mats Andrén, "Children's Laughter and Emotion Sharing With Peers and Adults in Preschool," *Frontiers in Psychology*, 10 (April 2019): 852, https:// doi.org/10.3389/fpsyg.2019.00852.

[5]Elton Trueblood, *The Humor of Christ: A Significant but Often Unrecognized Aspect of Christ's Teaching* (New York: Harper and Row, 1964), 22.

[6]Jim Gaffigan, "Best CATHOLIC Jokes Compilation," YouTube, August 30, 2020, www .youtube.com/watch?v=f5TPR2vFfZQ.

[7]Paige Davis, "How Children Develop a Sense of Humour," *The Conversation*, May 2, 2017, https://theconversation.com/how-children-develop-a-sense-of-humour -77028.

[8]Elizabeth-Anne Stewart, *Jesus the Holy Fool* (Franklin, WI: Sheed and Ward, 1999), 61.

[9]Dallas Willard, *Hearing God: Developing a Conversational Relationship With God* (Downers Grove, IL: InterVarsity Press, 1999), 38.

[10]His Holiness the Dalai Lama and Archbishop Desmond Tutu, with Douglas Abrams, *The Book of Joy: Lasting Happiness in a Changing World* (New York: Avery, 2016), 207.

[11]"'He Loved, He Laughed, He Cried': Desmond Tutu: In His Own Words," *Guardian*, video obituary, December 26, 2021, www.theguardian.com/world/video/2021/dec /26/desmond-tutu-in-his-own-words-video-obituary.

[12]Joan Chittister, *Radical Spirit: 12 Ways to Live a Free and Authentic Life* (New York: Convergent Books, 2017), 16.

[13]Jon Sweeney, *The St. Francis Holy Fool Prayer Book* (Brewster, MA: Paraclete, 2017).

[14]Trueblood, *Humor of Christ*, 54.

[15]*Steel Magnolias*, directed by Herbert Ross (Natchitoches, LA: Tri-Star Pictures, 1989).

[16]Archbishop Desmond Tutu and Mpho Tutu, edited by Douglas C. Abrams, *Made for Goodness: And Why This Makes All the Difference* (New York: Harper Collins, 2010), 108-47 (or do yourself a favor and read the whole book).

[17] Edward Hays, *Holy Fools and Mad Hatters: A Handbook for Hobbyhorse Holiness* (Leavenworth, KS: Forest of Peace, 1993), 37.

[18] Stewart, *Jesus the Holy Fool*, 206-7.

9. FREEDOM TO LEARN

[1] Rachel Wu, "Cognitive Benefits of Learning New Skills as an Older Adult," January 25, 2021, in *The Takeaway* podcast, WGBH www.wnycstudios.org /podcasts/takeaway/segments/cognitive-benefits-learning-new-skills-older-adult.

[2] *The Last Jedi*, directed by Rian Johnson (San Francisco: Lucasfilm, 2017).

[3] Tom Vanderbilt, *Beginners: The Joy and Transformative Power of Lifelong Learning* (London: Atlantic Books, 2021).

[4] Alison Gopnik, *Philosophical Baby: What Children's Minds Tell Us About Truth, Love and the Meaning of Life* (New York: Farrar, Straus and Giroux, 2009), 10.

[5] R. C. Sproul, "When Jesus Says, 'Be Ye Perfect as Your Father in Heaven Is Perfect,' Does That Mean We Can Attain Perfection, and Should We?" Ligonier, www .ligonier.org/learn/qas/when-jesus-says-be-ye-perfect-your-father-heaven-p/.

[6] Michael Harter, SJ, editor, *Hearts on Fire: Praying with the Jesuits* (Chicago: Loyola Press, 2004), 53.

[7] You can buy one for yourself at www.monasterygreetings.com/product/trappist -mug/all-gifts-mugs.

[8] Dallas Willard, *Renovation of the Heart: Putting on the Character of Christ* (Colorado Springs, CO: NavPress, 2002), 90-91.

10. PAY ATTENTION

[1] Phyllis Tickle, "The Request for Presence," in *The Divine Hours: Pocket Edition* (New York: Oxford University Press, 2007), 20.

[2] Macrina Wiederkehr, *Seven Sacred Pauses: Living Mindfully Through the Hours of the Day* (Notre Dame, IN: Sorin Books, 2008), 2.

CONCLUSION: BORN A MYSTIC

[1] Evelyn Underhill, *The Essentials of Mysticism* (Mansfield Centre, CT: Martino, 2013), 2.

[2] Peter M. Vishton, *Scientific Secrets for Raising Kids Who Thrive* (Chantilly, VA: The Great Courses, 2014).

[3] John O'Donohue, *Walking in Wonder: Eternal Wisdom for a Modern World* (New York: Convergent Books, 2015), 152-53.

[4] "Eternal Child," Roxy Humphrey, used with permission.